ORGANIZATIONAL TRANSITIONS: MANAGING COMPLEX CHANGE

ORGANIZATIONAL TRANSITIONS: MANAGING COMPLEX CHANGE

RICHARD BECKHARD

REUBEN T. HARRIS

Massachusetts Institute of Technology

ADDISON-WESLEY PUBLISHING COMPANY

Reading, Massachusetts • Menlo Park, California

London • Amsterdam • Don Mills, Ontario • Sydney

This book is in the Addison-Wesley series:

ORGANIZATION DEVELOPMENT

Editors:
Edgar H. Schein
Warren G. Bennis
Richard Beckhard

ISBN 0-201-00335-X
ABCDEFGHIJ-HC-7987

FOREWORD

It has been five years since the Addison-Wesley series on organization development published the books by Roeber, Galbraith, and Steele, and it is almost ten years since the series itself was launched in an effort to define the then-emerging field of organization development. Almost from its inception the series enjoyed a great success and helped to define what was then only a budding field of inquiry. Much has happened in the last ten years. There are now dozens of textbooks and readers on OD; research results are beginning to accumulate on what kinds of OD approaches have what effects; educational programs on planned change and OD are growing; and there are regional, national, and even international associations of practitioners of planned change and OD. All of these trends suggest that this area of practice has taken hold and found an important niche for itself in the applied social sciences and that its intellectual underpinnings are increasingly solidifying.

One of the most important trends we have observed in the last five years is the connecting of the field of planned change and OD to the mainstream of organization theory, organizational psychology, and organizational sociology. Although the field has its roots primarily in these underlying disciplines, it is only in recent years that basic textbooks in "organization behavior" have begun routinely referring to organization development as an applied area that students and managers alike must be aware of.

The editors of this series have attempted to keep an open mind on the question of when the series has fulfilled its function and should be allowed to die. The series should be kept alive only as long as new areas of knowledge and practice central to organization development are emerging. During the last year or so, several such areas have been defined, leading to the decision to continue the series.

On the applied side, it is clear that information is a basic nutrient for any kind of valid change process. Hence, a book on data gathering, surveys, and feedback methods is very timely. Nadler has done an especially important service in this area in focusing on the variety of methods which can be used in gathering information and feeding it back to clients. The book is eclectic in its approach, reflecting the fact that there are many ways to gather information, many kinds to be gathered, and many approaches to the feedback process to reflect the particular goals of the change program.

Team building and the appropriate use of groups continues to be a second key ingredient of most change programs. So far no single book in the field has dealt explicitly enough with this important process. Dyer's approach will help the manager to diagnose when to use and not use groups and, most important, how to carry out team building when that kind of intervention is appropriate.

One of the most important new developments in the area of planned change is the conceptualizing of how to work with large systems to initiate and sustain change over time. The key to this success is "transition management," a stage or process frequently referred to in change theories, but never explored systematically from both a theoretical and practical point of view. Beckhard and Harris present a model which will help the manager to think about this crucial area. In addition, they provide a set of diagnostic and action tools which will enable the change manager in large systems to get a concrete handle on transition management.

The area of organization design has grown in importance as organizations have become more complex. Davis and Lawrence provide a concise and definitive analysis of that particularly elusive organization design—the matrix organization—and elucidate clearly its forms, functions, and modes of operation.

Future volumes in the new series will explore the interconnections between OD and related areas which are becoming increasingly important to our total understanding of organizations, the process of management, and the nature of work. The whole quality-of-work-life area has spawned a growing concern with the nature of work itself and the context within which it occurs. Human-resource planning and career development are increasingly becoming organically linked to planned change programs. As people are discovering the variety of goals and aspirations which encompass different careers and life stages, more emphasis will have to be given to alternative work patterns and reward systems. All of these issues become even more complex in the multinational organization.

It is exciting to see our field develop, expand, strengthen its roots, and grow outward in many new directions. I believe that the core theory or the integrative framework is not yet at hand, but that the varied activities of the theoreticians, researchers, and practitioners of planned change and OD are increasingly relevant not only to the change manager, but also to line managers at all levels. As the recognition grows that part of *every* manager's job is to plan, initiate, and manage change, so will the relevance of concepts and methods in this area come to be seen as integral to the management process itself. It continues to be the goal of this series to provide such relevant concepts and methods to managers. I hope we have succeeded in some measure in this new series of books.

Cambridge, Massachusetts
June 1977

Edgar H. Schein

PREFACE

This book is addressed first to managers of change in large, complex organizations. It is addressed secondarily to those organization and management consultants whose profession and practice is to help executive managers in managing change.

We are assuming that today's executive managers, in addition to overseeing the operations of their organizations, are significantly concerned with managing the design and plan for the future of the organization and the management of the human, financial, technical, and other resources necessary to move from the present state of affairs to the desirable future state.

In the last few years, increasing environmental and task complexity have put increasing pressure on executive managers to focus more attention on managing this change process—"the transition state"—moving from today's condition to some desired future state. Concurrently, in the past few years, there has been developed considerable new technology and knowledge about how to manage this change process.

In this book we try to bring together, for the executive manager, an overview of the issues involved in diagnosing the organization, managing the transition, and managing the changed state. We hope to provide some guidelines to those who intervene in this process, whether as managers or as resources to the managers.

We have purposely focused on the subject from the point of view of the executive manager, not the consultant. However, in most of the cases mentioned in the book, one or both of us have been involved as resources, facilitating the change. To be effective, consultation has to include suggesting methods, providing expert help, translating theory into application to the specific organization problems, and suggesting tools for managing the process.

It is our hope that this book will help to clarify and put in some order the great variety of interventions and strategies managers are using to cope with this complex change process. We hope also that it will help in some way to make available to managers further information and understanding of the knowledge and technology that are available to help them as they engage in moving the organization through these transitions.

Cambridge, Mass.   R. B.
June 1977   R. T. H.

ACKNOWLEDGMENTS

We want to thank a few of the many whose energy and thoughts contributed to this book: our wives, Elaine and Tamara, who stayed with us and let it happen; our colleague, Ed Schein, who also stayed with us with sharp and friendly criticism—and helped it happen; and our secretary, Gloria Malkin, who typed and retyped and made it happen.

CONTENTS

1
THE CHANGING PRACTICE
OF ORGANIZATION DEVELOPMENT

Executive managers of contemporary complex organizations are currently and will increasingly find themselves faced with an expanding mix of demands for their time and energy. Few institutional leaders would argue against the view that the environment surrounding their organization is more turbulent and thus more uncertain than it was even a few years ago. Further, it appears that this increase in turbulence is increasing at an accelerating pace. The consequences of these changes in the world surrounding the organization are making it a whole new ball game for the executive manager.

It is not that the responsibilities of executive managers will change. They will continue to be—as they have always been —responsible for the effective operation of their organization. They will be responsible and accountable for the development of priorities, goals, and strategic plans for the future of the organization. They will be responsible for managing the conditions and activities that get the organization from its present state to some desired state. The changes in the role of the manager grow out of the matrix between these responsibilities and the complexity of choice and decision situations resulting from increasing variety of environmental demands on the organization. To paraphrase Harlan Cleveland (1972): The core problem of an executive manager in a complex organization is to make the best *choices* around whom to bring together, in which organizations, to make what happen, in whose interpretation of the public interest.[1]

Not too long ago, the *best choices* were relatively clear and straightforward. Today, and likely more so in the future, "best choice" selection will represent complex dilemmas in priorities and problem solving. For example, in trying to decide whether to spend extra capital in building a new plant in order to reduce the likelihood of polluting the environment or whether to put that capital back into the hands of the owners as a return on their investments, the chief executive or top-management group is facing this kind of dilemma. The same types of choice dilemmas are faced by the chief executive of an organization in deciding whether and how to maintain a position in a country where much of the wealth production is being nationalized—yet there is a place for this organization to do business in that country. Clearly the choices are not simple.

Further, the selection of the "best option" is only the first step. Due to the critical nature of the issues surrounding these choices, the "best option" is seldom one of continuing operations as usual. Rather, the choice is generally one that requires a significant change in organizational priorities and/or the way the organization goes about conducting its business and achieving its goals. Such changes—about definition of goals and priorities, organizational restructuring, modifying organization-environment relationships, and the like—all require significant and sustained involvement of top management.

Paralleling these changes in the demands surrounding executive managers and their organizations has been the emergence of new concepts, knowledge, and technologies relevant to the management of change in complex organizations. Let us look briefly at the nature of some of the changes in thinking about organizational change which have been evolving over the past several years.

THE CHANGING CHARACTER
OF ORGANIZATION DEVELOPMENT

In 1969, in an earlier book in this series, Beckhard defined organization development as "an effort (1) *planned*, (2) *organization-wide*,

---

1   H. Cleveland, *The Future Executive* (New York: Harper & Row, 1972), p. 140.

and (3) *managed* from the *top*, to (4) increase *organization effectiveness* and *health* through (5) *planned interventions* in the organization's 'processes,' using *behavioral-science* knowledge." [2] In the same book, organization health was defined as a series of organizational conditions, which are listed below:

a) The total organization, the significant subparts, and individuals, manage their work against *goals* and *plans* for achievement of these goals.

b) Form follows function (the problem, or task, or project, determines how the human resources are organized).

c) Decisions are made by and near the sources of information regardless of where these sources are located on the organization chart.

d) The reward system is such that managers and supervisors are rewarded (and punished) comparably for:

short-term profit or production performance,
growth and development of their subordinates,
creating a viable working group.

e) Communication laterally and vertically is *relatively* undistorted. People are generally open and confronting. They share all the relevant facts including feelings.

f) There is a minimum amount of inappropriate win/lose activities between individuals and groups. Constant effort exists at all levels to treat conflict and conflict-situations as *problems* subject to problem-solving methods.

g) There is high "conflict" (clash of ideas) about tasks and projects, and relatively little energy spent in clashing over *interpersonal* difficulties because they have been generally worked through.

h) The organization and its parts see themselves as interacting with each other *and* with a *larger* environment. The organization is an "open system."

---

2   R. Beckhard, *Organization Development: Strategies and Models* (Reading, Mass.: Addison-Wesley, 1969), p. 9.

i) There is a shared value, and management strategy to support it, of trying to help each person (or unit) in the organization maintain his (or its) integrity and uniqueness in an interdependent environment.

j) The organization and its members operate in an "action-research" way. General practice is to build in *feedback mechanisms* so that individuals and groups can learn from their own experience.[3]

The practice of organization development in 1969 for the most part involved activities intended to increase the effectiveness of some subpart of the organization, such as improving the ability of teams and groups to work together, helping develop better relationships between groups in an organization, increasing the effectiveness of the goal-setting process, increasing managerial skills at conflict management, etc. Rarely was an organization's OD effort an example of Beckhard's definition.

Since 1969, however, the priority concerns of executive managers have become increasingly consistent with the kinds of things implied in Beckhard's definition. It is increasingly necessary in today's complex organizations to have a planned, managed-from-the-top, organizationwide effort to create a set of conditions and a state that will allow the organization to "creatively" cope with the changing outside demands on it and that can also increase the possibility of organizational survival. Also, in recent years we have begun to see some significant changes in the practice of planned change—both in the way people think about it and in the technology.

The demands on organizations are becoming increasingly complex. Old assumptions about the stable state of an organization have of necessity been replaced with concerns about how to handle the "dynamics" while maintaining some degree of stability.

The executive manager needs knowledge, skills, and technology as never before to help in (1) understanding the present state of affairs in the organization, (2) developing relatively clear goals of where he or she wants the organization to get to in the intermediate future, (3) producing a fairly clear picture of a desired state to be achieved by some specified time, and (4) specifying a clear picture of the state which

---

3   *Ibid.*, pp. 10–11.

must exist during the interim. We will refer to this last state as the *transition state*. New experience and findings have emerged which, we believe, can help the organization to manage this state. Perhaps the most helpful point to be made is that rather than thinking of the time between the present state and some desired state as a period during which a *plan* must be made, it should be thought of as a *state of affairs* in itself, requiring a governance or a management structure and specific work plans and controls unique to that state.

For example, consider the situation in which it has been determined that there is a need to change the complete information system in a large hospital *from* one in which various types of information are maintained by different departments and transferred by messengers *to* a centralized computer-based multiple input-output information system capable of meeting all hospital information storage, retrieval, and transfer needs. Such a change will affect almost everyone who works in the hospital, and there will be significant implications for certain departments, e.g., medical records, business office, laboratories, and pharmacy, etc. The traditional approach to such a change would be to define a *plan* detailing how people and departments will behave and be organized *when* the change is *complete*. What is often not adequately recognized is that such a change will involve a significant period of time—a period that is significantly different from the prechange state (present) and from the postchange state (future). During this transition state, people are dismantling the old system and learning how to make the new system work—how the new structures operate, how the computer system operates—learning new skills and new role relationships, and operating simultaneously with both systems, etc. The transition period is a dynamic yet unique state of affairs, one that requires significant management attention and planning.

Since 1969, we have also witnessed changes in the technology of planned change. The technology used to help organization leaders in the area of planned change has moved from an emphasis on team building and intergroup relationships and the like to an emphasis on developing planning processes for coping with the organization and its environment, developing methods of designing and managing new organizational structures, e.g., matrix structures, looking at new techniques for managing complex role interactions where responsibility is widely distributed and for deciding the structure and procedures for managing the transition state, and developing new systems for analyzing and taking a better picture of the present state of an organization. In essence, the focus of planned-change technologies has shifted from an orientation of primarily human-resource development to one of more comprehensive system development. At the basis of this latter perspective is the view of an organization as a complex set of interdependent subsystems—people, structures, technology, tasks—which are embedded in a dynamic environment and recognition of the need for developing and maintaining compatibility among these subsystems.[4]

The emphasis on systemwide technologies and the concept of the "transition state" represent the kinds of shifts in thinking about the process of change in complex systems which has been occurring in recent years. It is these new ways of looking at and managing the change process which will form the basis of this book.

ORGANIZATION OF THIS BOOK

Chapter 2 looks at some issues in the environment today and tries to provide a perspective for the changing nature of the organization world and some implications for managing change. The next four chapters deal with various aspects of "transition management," or managing the change process. Chapter 3 begins by trying to take an accurate picture of the present state and developing a clear picture of the desired future state. We then present a model for organizational diagnosis, give some illustrations from practice, and look at the kinds of action implications growing out of the diagnosis.

Chapter 4 looks at management structures and processes in the transition state. We examine some alternative ways of organizing and managing transitions, look at some techniques for developing plans for change, and consider in some detail the issues and alternative models for getting the commitment necessary for an effective change to occur in a complex system.

---

4   *See* H. J. Leavitt, *Managerial Psychology,* 3rd ed. (Chicago: University of Chicago Press, 1972), pp. 259–265; W. G. Ouchi and R. T. Harris, "Structure, Technology, and Environment," in G. Strauss *et al.*, eds., *Organizational Behavior: Research and Issues* (Belmont, Cal.: Wadsworth, 1976).

In Chapter 5 we explore criteria for choosing an intervention strategy. A significant issue is the freedom of choice the manager has pertaining to the change. We look at the difference in implications and consequences between conditions under which the manager can choose *whether* and *how* to make the change and those under which the only choice available is how to make the change. We examine the issue of where in the system to intervene and suggest some criteria for choosing among alternative interventions.

Some specific intervention technologies—the applications of behavioral science disciplines and knowledge to specific classes of change problems—are considered in Chapter 6. We look at organizations and their relationships to the environment, discuss open-systems planning as a technology, and give some illustrations of applications of this model to organizational change problems. We also look at some questions of changing organizational structure and designing and managing matrix structures, again providing cases and illustrations. Finally, we look at the problem of managing interfaces within and between organizations and detail a technology for working with these conflicts.

Chapter 7 explores alternative purposes and what's involved in the evaluation of a change effort. The purpose of this chapter is to give to the change management and the consultant an overview of what is possible in an evaluation effort and to suggest some preliminary guidelines for designing and carrying out an evaluation plan.

Chapter 8 looks at the crucial problems facing organizational managers, who must maintain or stabilize a change state and also handle the dilemma of the simultaneous need for both flexibility and stability. We discuss some ways of keeping in tune with the organization in its new state and suggest several alternative management structures for ensuring both self-renewal and stability.

Chapter 9 presents a brief look at the future—the kinds of change problems that will probably be facing executive managers and the kinds of help they will probably need.

2
THE DEMANDING WORLD OF THE MANAGER

In this chapter, we want to take a broad look at the nature of the organizational world—identifying some of the forces affecting contemporary organizations and their leaders. It is not our intent to engage in a detailed discussion of the nature of these environmental demands. Other authors have observed and described these dynamics elsewhere.[1] Rather, we will outline the nature of the demands and point out their implications for management and change. As we noted in Chapter 1, the organizational world of today is much more dynamic and complex than that of the 1960s, and it will probably become more so rather than less so in the future. It is our view that in order to effectively manage complex systems in today's world, the organizational leader must have some basic understanding of the nature of the environmental forces affecting his or her actions and outcomes.

The Increasingly Complex Pressures on Organizational Leaders

The number of major forces requiring changes in organizations' priorities and activities is significantly larger in the 1970s than it was in the

---

1 *See* R. J. C. Roeber, *The Organization in a Changing Environment* (Reading, Mass.: Addison-Wesley, 1973); E. Schein, *Human Resource Planning and Career Development: Some New Perspectives* (Reading, Mass.: Addison-Wesley, 1977).

1960s. Witness the changes required by new technological developments and increased task complexity. In addition, in the last ten years, and particularly in the last five, the problems of changing social priorities and changing economic requirements have required executive managers to make major choices about both their organizations' *mission* and *social* priorities.

Organization leaders must respond to the following kinds of demands: multiple constituencies, constraints from the outside environment, changing values in society, changing values of employees, and increasing complexity of tasks. Let's look at each of these briefly.

THE MULTIPLE CONSTITUENCIES OF THE MANAGER

Organization leaders have been and are continually "losing control" over the organizations they manage. Constraints from the outside environment, changing demands from employees and staffs, and changing values have necessitated reordering priorities and redefining the autonomy of an enterprise. For example, if one had asked the president of a business organization a few years ago, "For whom are you steward; to whom are you primarily responsible?" the answer would have been simple and clear: "the owners, the stockholders, the banks." Decisions could then be made on the basis of whose interest must be served first. Organization managers also felt responsibilities to employees and in a general way to society at large. In the public sector, the priorities were reversed, in the sense that the public at large could be viewed as the primary constituency or owners; the employees, a secondary constituency.

Today, however, the response of the president of a business organization would be much more hesitant. Today's president still has a primary responsibility to the owners, but also experiences an almost equal responsibility to other constituencies. For example, suppose we can build a plant for a million dollars. The plant will be 100 percent cost-effective—an ideal of efficiency. An alternative is to build the same plant for two million dollars; it will be somewhat less cost-effective in the use of the owners' money, but it won't pollute anything for ten years. What criteria does the president use to decide whether to spend one million, one and a half million, or two million of the owners' money on the plant? If responsibility to the owners for their investment were still the dominant criterion, the decision would be easy. But because of the consequences of a decision of this kind on the marketplace, on public attitudes toward the organization, etc., the president may well decide to be less than fully cost-effective. The final decision, however, will be one that, after risk-analysis, is a very personal one, based on a weighing of the relative potency of the demands of the various constituencies for whom the president is *now* steward. The critical question is: What criteria does the manager use in determining a course of action? Furthermore, what demands does the manager respond to?

Whatever choices are made, the manager's power to control the outcomes has been severely constrained. We suspect that in the years immediately ahead, these constraints and complexities will become greater rather than less.

DEMANDS FROM THE OUTSIDE ENVIRONMENT

One can classify the outside environmental demands as follows:

1. Increasing controls from government agencies and regulatory bodies;

2. Increasing social pressures by citizen groups;

3. Increasing legal constraints through new legislation;

4. Increasing social constraints through pressures by consumer groups, environmentalists, etc.;

5. Increasing constraints by interdependent institutions, such as unions, etc.

Behind all of these types of constraints are the worldwide changes in societal values and priorities which are affecting organizations across national, cultural, economic, and political boundaries. For example, the role of economic enterprises is being challenged throughout the world. Is the fundamental role of a business organization to produce wealth? If it is, for whom—the owners? the commonwealth? the government?

In a number of countries today, one finds that the dominant value, in many cases backed by government legislation, concerning the role of economic enterprise is that the core mission—the reason for being—is to provide employment. Picture yourself as the general manager of a multinational corporation located in Ireland or Germany or Scandinavia, where the role of the enterprise is defined as being an employment provider. The demand of the owners is to provide return on investment to them. If you are trying to become more efficient as well as more effective and to cut costs and perhaps reduce employment, you find yourself up against legislation prohibiting it. Whom do you please? Whose side are you on? Legislation emerging throughout the European Common Market and Scandinavia requires the policy direction of a private enterprise to be in the hands of both owners and employees, and in some cases public representatives as well. Thus we see the emergence of a two-tiered board of directors whose membership is composed of owner-representatives, employee-representatives, and in some cases the public. Such a board has the power to hire and fire the chief executive and to make major policy decisions. The degree of freedom provided to the organizational leaders under this set of conditions is very different from that in a traditional set of conditions.

In the public sector of the United States, we can see endless examples of this new set of conditions. National health policy and priorities are matters of concern to most legislators today. The increasing intervention of the federal government into the policies of medical education and practice produces severe constraints on organization leaders in these fields. Demands for educational equality, backed up by legal statutes and in some cases by the militia, set new constraints and demands on the leaders of school systems.

CHANGING VALUES

Anyone in a position of organization leadership today has experienced the problems connected with changing values, not only societal, but among employees and staffs as well. In the United States, the increasing concern and action regarding the rights of minorities and women are having heavy impact on organization policies and practices. In response to the legislation "demanding" equal opportunity and affirmative action programs, many organizations have developed a "compliance strategy." The underlying postures are probably either "to do as little as we can to stay out of jail" or "to do whatever is done by our group of industries, universities, or organizations." Both of these postures have been effective in recent years because of limited enforcement provisions. However, both of these postures are likely to be self-destructive to the organization in the long run, since pressures are likely to increase for active programs of equal opportunity. The development of a managerial strategy that takes an active position has tremendous implications for the organization's policies, procedures, and money. It costs considerably more in personnel investment. It requires considerably more in follow-up.

In the late 1960s, we saw the organizational consequences resulting from the changing youth values toward work expectations, needs for participation, loyalty to the organization, etc. Much of the "noise" that grew out of this energy has quieted down considerably in the last few years, but the changed values are there and need to be taken into account by organization leaders.

One of the major spinoffs of the 1960s is occurring with the parents of these youths—people in their forties, many of whom are tending to examine critically the "matrix" between their work and non-work lives. Middle managers and executives are beginning to ask: What are the plusses of working until age 65 versus working part-time and developing a second career? As children leave home earlier, psychologically if not physically, nonworking wives are saying to their working husbands, "For the rest of our lives, we have only each other, and you have new responsibilities to me."

In addition, as the United States moves toward national health insurance and transferable pension plans and as the view of retirement as commencement rather than as death becomes more prevalent, people in managerial roles in organizations now have many more choices about what to do with the rest of their lives. The old societal values of the Protestant work ethic that rewarded a person for working 60 or 80 hours a week have been replaced with generally shared norms that there are other valued ways of living. After many years of affluence, increasing taxation, and opportunities for more leisure, more and more middle managers are reexamining their whole work careers and actively considering early retirement or a change in their work status. This has tremendous consequences for all sorts of organizational practices, e.g., promotions and career planning and the types of reward systems.[2]

For example, in trying to meet this changing set of demands, one organization has developed three benefits plans for its management staff, each of which cost the organization about the same amount of money. Annually, every management person can choose which of the three plans to be covered by. One of these plans is bonus-based, and another one allows an extended vacation or sabbatical. It is possible, therefore, for someone to trade a bonus for an extended leave in a particular year. This particular personnel practice has had significant effects on reducing the concerns of many of its management people about their careers and life plans.

INCREASING COMPLEXITY OF TASKS

As the complexity of tasks has increased in recent years, the need for new forms of organizing work and new organizational structures has also increased. Most simple organizations operate effectively with functional organization structures based on technologies, such as sales or production, or disciplines, such as internal medicine or pediatrics in a medical school. As the organization's tasks become more differentiated, however, it is often necessary to create program or project organizations, in which a variety of different technologies are combined within one program. Examples are a business area within a larger organization based on a particular market or product, such as the commercial paints organization within a large chemical firm or a community health center within a large academic medical institution.

---

2   For an in-depth discussion of the issues surrounding this phenomenon of the manager's changing perspective on work and the resulting organizational consequences, *see* L. Bailyn and E. H. Schein, "Life/Career Considerations as Indicators of Quality of Employment," in A. D. Biderman and T. F. Drury, eds., *Measuring Work Quality for Social Reporting* (New York: Sage/Wiley, 1976); R. Beckhard, "The Executive You're Counting on May Be Ready to Mutiny," *Innovation*, No. 31, May 1972; J. Van Maanen and E. H. Schein, "Improving the Quality of Working Life: Career Development," in J. R. Hackman and L. Suttle, eds., *Improving Life at Work* (Los Angeles: Goodyear, 1976).

All sorts of new dilemmas grow out of this condition. For example, if an organization does business worldwide, is leadership based on area, having regional geographic management, or on products, with worldwide product management, or on technologies? How do the three relate? What criteria does one use? Similarly, if a large medical center made up of several hospitals and a medical school decides to develop more community health delivery sites, does one organize these community centers under a project director, or does one locate the sites in one of the existing departments, such as medicine or pediatrics?

If it is decided that instead of statewide or regional special schools for the handicapped, every local community must provide a complete elementary education for *all* the children in the community, how does one reorganize the elementary schools? Does one have a special department for the handicapped or special classrooms, or does one change the curriculum so that everybody can take the same courses at the same time?

In many organizations, neither the old functional organization based on technology nor the program or project organization based on mission provides a satisfactory answer. In order to allocate scarce resources to a variety of projects and to maintain technical quality, it is often necessary to assign people to two different areas, to both a program and a functional or technical area. When this happens, we have the beginnings of a *matrix* condition, in which the individual belongs in two "homerooms"—perhaps reports to two bosses and has to make a whole new set of choices concerning his or her work priorities.

The complexity of tasks requires, in many situations, new governing instructions, new coordinating mechanisms, the installation of new information systems, and new methods and techniques for defining responsibility. These changes, as well as the other changes outlined earlier, require comprehensive planning and sophisticated strategies involving an analysis of alternatives and consequences, financial and time investments, a conscious decision about how to manage the program, and decisions about how to monitor and control the program's development. Such a program cannot be put into effect or maintained by simply creating a staff of specialists or sending out orders to comply, as most executive managers have discovered. It is a far more complex issue of planning, requiring personal investment of the senior executives, diagnosis of the total system, and plans for getting "ownership" of the changes on the part of many people.

CONCLUSION

As a result of changes in the state of the organizational world, there is an increasing concern with the management of change and need for effective strategies for large-system change. We define a large-system change strategy as a *plan* defining what *interventions* to make *where*, by *whom*, and at what *time* in order to move the organization to a state where it can optimally *transform* needs into results in a social environment that nurtures people's worth and dignity. Managerially, this means defining the kinds of activities that need to be induced and the kinds of expertise that need to be brought to bear to help with the change; identifying people in the organization who need to become committed to the change; establishing a timetable and specifying priorities of changes and practices in procedures, rewards, policies, and behavior; establishing a system of evaluating progress toward a new state; and providing education in skills needed to both operate in the new condition and manage the change.

The choice of whether or not to be concerned about a large-system change strategy is virtually removed from operating managers of complex enterprises. The changing and increasingly complex environment around organizations, the changing values and demands of employees in organizations, the changing expectations and demands of users of the organization's products and services—all require that organization leaders now begin developing strategies for coping with these demands and managing for organizational survival as well as for growth.

3
DEFINING THE PRESENT AND THE FUTURE

The change process in a large complex institutional system has several aspects:

1. Diagnosing the present condition, including the need for change;

2. Setting goals and defining the new state or condition after the change;

3. Defining the transition state between the present and the future;

4. Developing strategies and action plans for managing this transition;

5. Evaluating the change effort;

6. Stabilizing the new condition and establishing a balance between stability and flexibility.

In this chapter, we focus on the issues involved in (1) diagnosing the present organizational condition as it relates to a need for change and (2) defining the desired "end state." We will first examine some methods of assessing the need for change and then look at how one can develop early descriptions of the end state. The rest of the chapter describes a set of diagnostic steps for producing a clear picture of the present state of affairs, as well as the data needed for planning an action strategy for changing it. We will briefly review some methods of analyzing a change problem; analyze the processes necessary to be changed, such as attitudes and policies; look at some types of change goals; and look at a method of analyzing the subsystems in the organization and some methods for determining first action steps.

There are two essential conditions for any change effort to be effectively managed. First, the organization leadership must be aware of the need for change and its consequences for their actions. Second, a desired end state must be relatively explicit; that is, the organization leadership must have a relatively clear idea of the changed condition desired. We contend that prerequisites for action planning and change strategy are: (1) a good diagnosis of a set of conditions causing a need for change; (2) a detailed picture of a desired end state; and (3) a clear and accurate picture of the dynamics of the present.

DEFINING THE NEED FOR CHANGE

The forces requiring change in large systems today tend to originate *outside* the organization. Changes in legislation, market demand, and social priorities frequently necessitate that organization managers redesign their organization structures, redefine their priorities, and reallocate resources. To clarify, consider the following illustrations.

1. The federal government of the United States has required that all organizations doing business with the government have affirmative action programs and specific action plans. To meet program goals, these plans must incorporate certain allocations of positions at all levels of the organization to females and minorities, in some specified relationship to the population distribution. The sanctions against organizations not having these affirmative action plans are significant in terms of the threat of loss of contracts with the government. Any organization leader faced with this condition is required to make some significant changes in reallocation of resources, training programs, recruitment policies, and promotion and payment policies. Although there are many choices about how to implement the program, the need for the change is significant and has immediate consequences.

2. A national priority in the United States is for more training of doctors to do primary care, or direct patient care, and also for more emphasis on preventive health care. A maldistribution of general prac-

titioners and an overproduction of specialists have caused policy makers to legislate that there shall be a different allocation of graduates from medical school and a different distribution of specialties. For the manager of a medical school, medical center, or hospital, the need for change, determined from the outside, is obvious and has, again, some major implications for the organization. The manager cannot ignore this pressure.

3.   Another form of pressure for change in the medical establishment comes from within. Traditionally, residents and interns have worked 80 to 120 hours a week in order to provide the coverage required by their teaching hospitals and to achieve their educational objectives. Now they are demanding that their work week be reduced. In determining an action response, the institutional manager must assess this force, the economic requirements of the institution, society's requirements, and the educational requirements for preparing physicians.

In each of these illustrations, the pressure for change arises external to the management structure, and any action response or lack of response has significant consequences.

What Needs Changing? Differentiating Causes and Symptoms

Frequently, the change problem is described in "symptoms" terms. One important consequence of a good organizational diagnosis is an accurate statement of the change problem—something that is often lacking initially. For example, if the problem were defined as poor morale in a department or throughout the organization or as poor communication between the field offices and the headquarters, it would seem to follow that the needed change strategy should try to improve morale through some satisfaction-improvement activities or a communications-improvement program. Such strategies can work if the symptom statement describes the *fundamental* condition needing change.

A "more likely to succeed" strategy, however, would follow a diagnosis of those symptom description statements and ask "why." This would require diagnosing what might be causing the problems of morale or communications. For example, a school superintendent in a large school system stated that there was a morale problem among th teachers in the district and that something must be done to improve morale. Implicit in this statement of need was a goal statement that if morale improved, something would be significantly better in the system. The diagnostic questions in this instance are: "What would be different or better?" and "How much does it matter?" If the answer to the first question were that higher morale or an increase in the teachers' level of satisfaction would improve students' reading levels, there would be one set of choices. If the answer were that teachers would not call in sick so often if morale were improved, that would be another issue. If an improvement in students' reading levels were the goal rationale, the diagnosis would focus on the "causes" of the low reading levels. If a lower absentee rate for teachers were the goal rationale, the focus would be on understanding why teachers are using their sick leave. In each of these situations, what *needs* changing is not simply teachers' morale, but some other organizational condition.

DETERMINING THE DESIRED STATE

To return to the example about the affirmative action legislation, the problem for the organization management is to determine, based on an analysis of the forces in the situation and the leaders' own preferences, values, and sense of stewardship, the goals to be achieved in terms of the employment of females and minorities. To set a desired end state and describe it in explicit terms will subsume some value posture. For example, if the goals set are significantly above the government-defined minimums and if plans are developed to mobilize the resources to meet those goals, there is an obvious implication of an action-oriented strategy, and this has managerial consequences—for structure, for how rewards are distributed, and so forth.

On the other hand, the goal set may be to do the minimum amount of affirmative action planning necessary to meet legislative requirements. In other words, the goal may be to have a compliance strategy operating in the future, which will keep the organization "out of trouble." Thus with this goal the implications for the development of a change strategy will be quite different.

Obviously, setting goals and defining the problem are interlinked. We are saying that both should be *explicit*. We are also saying that it is important to recognize that although the concern for change is often triggered by the existence of some need or set of problem symptoms, it is the *goals set by the management* which should be the determining criteria for defining both the strategy and direction of change.

A Picture of the Future

We have found that it frequently helps organization managers to define the future state by developing a scenario, or extended wide-angle "photograph," of what the organization would look like in its new state. For example, if one were to take a picture of the new condition of the affirmative action situation, what would be happening? What would the policies be? What would the practices be? What kinds of training would be occurring? What would be the mix of personnel at that point?

If one were looking at a change in the emphasis of the delivery of health care from one of furthering the development of specialists to one of increasing general practice and family practice, what would the new condition look like? How many doctors would exist, and what would they be doing? What would be included in the medical school's curriculum?

If one is talking about a reallocation of power between owners' representatives and union or employee representatives in the management of an organization, what would this look like operationally? What decisions would be made, and how would they be made? How would major financial allocations be determined?

In short, we are suggesting that management develop a detailed description of what the organization will look like when the desired condition is achieved. This description should specify the expected organizational structure, reward system, personnel policies, authority and task-responsibility distributions, managerial styles and roles, performance-review systems, and performance outcomes. Ideally, this "wide-angle" view will be a comprehensive description of the future state. However, the key point is that a *detailed* picture should be produced, be it a "snapshot" or a "movie." Defining explicitly what the organization would look like in the new state serves as a descriptive guide for determining the change strategy. When coupled with an assessment of the present state, this "picture" of the future condition provides the information necessary for management to develop realistic action plans and timetables for managing the change.

DEFINING THE PRESENT SYSTEM

It is important, we believe, to go back and look at the present system before determining an action plan to achieve relatively explicit goals. Experience has shown that organizations and their managements often make erroneous assumptions about the current state of the organization when developing change strategies. The consequence of such a mistake is that the action plans developed assume a different current organizational condition than actually exists. The result of then implementing those action plans is likely to be confusion, frustration, unexpected resistance, and generally a failure to achieve the desired goal. To guard against such an outcome, management needs to develop a clear and accurate "picture" of the current state of the system. As in defining the nature of the desired future state, what is needed is a diagnosis of the system's current, and recent, structure and method of operating.

One of the first steps in looking at the system is to look at what parts of the system are most significantly involved in the change process and what changes in their present attitudes or behavior or ways of work would probably have to occur if the desired goal were to be reached. This means thinking about the total organization as it relates to the change goal. Thus a key question for the change management to answer first is: Which specific subunits would be primarily affected by the change?

A related set of questions deals with the types of processes which would need to be changed in order for the change to be effective. These processes or variables that need to be examined include: changes of attitudes required, changes of practices required, changes of policies required, changes of structures required, and changes of rewards required.

For example, there is tremendous and increasing concern all over the world today about improving the quality of the working environment. The social values of significant numbers of people throughout the world are changing toward increasing autonomy, more influence over working conditions, more dignity and freedom; all are requiring organization managements to give significant attention to the quality of the work environment.

Let us suppose that the management of an organization desires to significantly change the working environment in its manufacturing organizations. The desired end state is for people on the various production lines to actively design their own work processes, along with the technical experts; the way the work is done and the physical environment in which it is done would be developed by both the designers and the doers of the work. Let us suppose further that this change would mean a drastic change in production processes. For example, instead of people doing one piece of work on a production line, the work force might be organized into units or cells, each responsible for a total product. The diagnostic question is: What types of changes from the present way of doing things would be required? In this instance, one would have to change (1) the technical process, (2) decision making about the organization of work, (3) the reward or compensation systems, (4) the attitudes of supervisors about their own and the workers' jobs, (5) the practices governing the flow of materials and work, and (6) the decision-making authority for determining conditions of work among the workers, managers, and the unions.

The key questions confronting the organizational management include: Which of these changes would require priority attention? Is there some "domino effect" inherent in these changes? What needs to be done first? The following is a case history of such an organizational diagnosis and the action implications which grow out of the process.

Illustration

A multiplant manufacturing organization with plants in several countries was committed to improving the quality of working life. For a number of years, the organization had conducted experiments in organization design and redesign which provided more worker participation in the plants' organization and management and involved new systems of pay, work design, and governance. A new plant was to be built in a European country, and the new plant's product involved high, though already well-developed, technology in the manufacturing process. The plant would open with an American management group at the top, but as soon as possible the plant would operate with an almost entirely indigenous management and work force.

In defining the desired state after the opening of the plant, the project management looked at the technical process of manufacturing the product, the physical environment in which the product was manufactured, and the cultural environment of doing that work in a country whose social conditions were very different from those of the country in which the parent company was located. Six subsystems critical in this change were identified: (1) the manufacturing management, (2) the management group in the country where the plant would be located and where there were already some ongoing activities, (3) the plant manager, (4) the operating management group, (5) the first-line leadership, and (6) the managers' families.

Since, in its initial years, the plant would have a multicultural management group, with Americans in the top leadership positions in an unfamiliar culture and with everyone working with what was for them a new technology, it was decided that the change strategy would have to include:

1. Teaching the new technology to both the Americans and to the total management group from the host country;

2. Creating a new community in which people from both countries could work together in the host country;

3. Developing a common technical language with the same meanings in the host country and the home office;

4. Developing a living environment so that workers and their families would be relatively comfortable in the new situation;

5. Dealing with the many cross-cultural issues by specifically finding some ways of creating a learning community and a living community.

This diagnosis of the various systems involved and the gross needs of types of changes required formed the basis for the change strategy implemented. In brief, the change strategy included:

1. Learning the technical process in an existing plant in the parent company's environment:
   a) The members of the management group in the country where the new plant would be located and the temporary team of Americans who would be opening the plant spent up to a year with their families in a plant location learning the process.
   b) Technical manuals were translated by people who would ultimately be managing in the plant rather than by technical writers.

2. Providing the basis for each management group's learning the other's language:
   a) Managers and their families from the host country learned English, and members of the start-up team learned the other language.

3. Adapting to different living conditions:
   a) Families from the plant country lived in the United States, rented apartments and houses and bought or rented furniture, existing in a condition of adapting their life-style to the environmental conditions of this country for a short period of time.
   b) Members of the American team participated in this process and then moved to the host country, where they faced the same cultural and social adjustments.
   c) Types of housing, location of housing in relation to schools, and choice of language were the types of issues discussed and decided prior to relocation.

Appropriate systems as targets for change, then, may be the organization hierarchy or pieces of it, both inside and outside the formal structure, e.g., the participants' families, and in the organization's external environment. A conscious identification of the subsystems primarily affected by this particular change helps both reduce the number of subsystems to be considered and clarify directions for the strategy.

Determining Each Subsystem's "Readiness"
and "Capability" for the Change

An assessment of the readiness of the various subsystems is an analysis of the *attitudes* of these systems toward the change. In the illustration above, the management's assessment covered many areas: the readiness of manufacturing management for this major experiment, the readiness of the American plant managers to engage in a nontraditional process, the attitudes of the recruits for management positions in the host country toward relocating in order to learn a management job in a new plant, the families' attitudes toward this major disruption in their way of life, and so forth.

In addition to the attitudes of those involved, their *capability* to make the change should also be examined. Let us suppose that the training manager in an organization feels that there is a strong need to introduce a management-development program into the system in order to develop middle managers. Let us also suppose that organizational approval and the support of both the top executive officers and the line general managers are needed in order for the program to really "go." The training manager could analyze the relevant subsystems—the chief executive, the line managers, and the middle managers who would be involved in the program—to determine which of the appropriate systems to consider. The training manager too might be a relevant subsystem.

Having identified the systems, the training manager might then assess them against the individuals' readiness and capability relative to this change. For example, the assessment that the personnel director is strongly enthusiastic about and supportive of the program would be rated as high readiness. On the same criterion, by contrast, the chief executive might feel that management training is an acceptable, though low-priority activity and that it certainly should not tie up or use major resources, either financial or people. Feeling that management training is desirable but not central to the organization's effort, the chief executive would be rated as having low readiness.

On the capability measure, however, the personnel director may have no budget to support such an effort, whereas the chief executive officer could release funds easily. Thus the chief executive officer would have low readiness and high capability, and the personnel director would have high readiness and low capability. In developing a strategy for change, therefore, the training director would have to think through how to either increase the readiness of the chief executive in the hope that this would release the funds or find some way of increasing the capability of the personnel director to provide the resources necessary to support the program.

One other way of looking at readiness for change and the attitudes and motivation toward implementing change is to think in terms of the cost of changing. David Gleicher has developed a simple formula for determining this cost:

$$C = (ABD) > X,$$

where C = change, A = level of dissatisfaction with the status quo, B = clear desired state, D = practical first steps toward the desired state, and X = cost of change. In other words, there has to be enough dissatisfaction with the current state of affairs (A) for someone to be mobilized for the change. The various subsystems need to have clear enough goals (B); otherwise, the "cost" (X) is too high. For each subsystem, there needs to be some awareness of practical first steps (D) to move, if movement is to take place.

An early diagnosis to determine which of these conditions is not strong enough often provides direct clues as to where to put intervention energy. For example, if most of the system is not really dissatisfied with the present state of affairs, interventions should probably aim toward increasing the level of dissatisfaction. On the other hand, if there is plenty of dissatisfaction with the present state but no clear picture of what a desired state may be, early interventions might be aimed at getting strategic parts of the organization to define and clarify the ideal or desired state. If both of these conditions exist but practical first steps are missing, early interventions may well be to pick some subsystem, such as the top unit or a couple of pilot groups, to begin experimenting with various improvement activities.

Let us consider the following case illustration. A general manager was concerned because line managers were not making good use of staff resources. The general manager felt that the staff specialists were not aggressive enough in offering their help and that the line people, due to their need for autonomy and running their own shows, were not aware of or willing to use the help that was available. The general manager wanted to change this and was willing to personally manage this change until the staff and the line had started communicating with each other better and using each other's resources to solve business problems. After talking to both the line and staff leaders about this concern, the general manager set up a system whereby all staff specialists were to make field visits to all of the line locations, analyze the kinds of problems that could use staff resources, and develop some priorities with the field management in order to set action plans for further interaction. The staff people were to report back to the general manager after the field visits and to do so regularly over the next six months.

The staff followed the orders and visited the field operations; they had meetings, a few of which were productive, the rest frustrating; they came back to headquarters. In the meantime, the general manager had become very busy with some other priorities and was not able to or did not hold the planned follow-up meetings. After one round of visits, the staff stopped its visits except in those rare cases where the original meetings had been highly productive. Things returned to "normal."

Using the Gleicher formula in investigating this with the general manager, we discovered and he discovered that although he had been dissatisfied with the status quo and had a very clear picture of what he wanted to do and had instituted some practical first steps to carry out the change, he was not in fact *that* dissatisfied. He felt this was a condition that should be changed, but was prepared to put in enough energy only to start the change, not to continue to invest his personal energy through the follow-up reporting and to manage the change. When he became aware of the connection between his own medium level of dissatisfaction and the lack of "take in the situation, he reinstituted the follow-up reporting, and the change "took."

SUMMARY

For an effective change strategy to be developed, it is first essential to adequately diagnose the need for change. A second prerequisite for developing a change strategy is to set clear and explicit descriptions of the desired state of affairs after the change. A third necessity is to have a clear picture of the present state of affairs as related to the change goals. The picture, or diagnosis, of the organization's present state needs to include an identification of those subsystems that are primarily involved in the change, the attitudes of those systems and their leaders toward the change, their readiness to commit themselves to the change, and an objective assessment of their capability to do it. In addition, it is helpful to look at the types of change problems that will be involved in developing the strategy.

The period of time and the state of affairs that exists between an identification of need and the achievement of a desired future state can be thought of as the transition state. The next several chapters will explore this transition state, how it needs to be managed, the structural implications, and alternative strategies for getting from here to there.

4
THE TRANSITION STATE

Most organizational changes occur over a period of time, e.g., a business changing its method of going to market, a medical center changing its priorities in delivery, an institution reallocating jobs to meet equal opportunity requirements for minorities. In such instances, the organization management must devise a strategy for coping with the confusion of roles, decision making, and authority that will occur during the "transition period." The important issues to be considered in designing such a strategy include:

1. Determining the degree of *choice* about whether to change;

2. Determining *what* needs changing;

3. Determining *where* to intervene;

4. Choosing *intervention technologies*.

As in any decision-making process, the better the input information, the more likely the decision will be appropriate and effective. We will deal with each of these dimensions by identifying several types of questions, the answers to which provide the basis of the choice of an appropriate intervention strategy.

WHAT DEGREE OF CHOICE EXISTS ABOUT WHETHER TO CHANGE?

An apparently obvious, but very often overlooked, question is whether the leadership in the organization can decide *whether* to make a change or only *how* to make it. Before deciding on an intervention strategy, the manager needs to determine the amount of control or influence he or she has over the causes or conditions providing the stimulus for changing in the first place.

Some demands or sets of forces coming from outside the organization provide a requirement for a change. In that case, the organization leadership has no choice but to *cope* with the *demand* for change. Examples are legislation on environmental pollution or employment of minorities, legislation changing the allocation of physicians and distribution of medical students, new laws providing for educational parity for handicapped children, import regulations limiting product sales in a particular area, and successful union demands for new benefits or new power.

In other situations, the need for change is stimulated by forces either internal or external to the organization, but nonetheless under management's general control, e.g., the need for reorganization because of a reorientation from a technical organization to a more marketing-oriented one, the need for adding a new department or teaching content in a medical school, the demand for increasing participation of students in the university decisions or of workers in managing work in a production line or of managers for professional development, the need for increased centralization of power, and the need to introduce new planning procedures or computers or other technology. In these types of conditions, the manager can choose not only *how* to initiate, implement, and carry out the change, but also *whether* to initiate the change.

It might be useful to think of the dilemma as a kind of grid (see Fig. 4.1). On one axis we can list the *sources* of the forces pressing on the management that are pushing toward a change, such as owners/directors, legislators, employees, trade unions, special-interest and pressure groups, and social values. On the other axis we can identify the *potency* of the force—high, medium, or low. Management can then array the nature of the forces operating in the situation by first

Nature of change demanded: _____

Potency of Forces	Forces Pushing Toward a Change	Owners	Legistlature	Employees	Trade Unions	Social Values
HIGH						
MEDIUM						
LOW						

Fig. 4.1 Example of grid for analyzing the sources and potency of forces for change.

specifying the nature of the change demanded and then identifying the potency of the demands for change, if any, being made by each "source." Additionally, the forces for or against the change can be designated with plus (+) or minus (−) signs, respectively. Such a display provides some perspective about what has to be taken into account before making any decisions about an action *strategy*.

Case Illustration 1: External Forces for Change; No Choice about Whether to Make the Change

The country manager of a multinational organization was faced with a dilemma. The mayors of two major cities in the host country had issued proclamations declaring it a crime for citizens to purchase the type of product that his company and his competitors sold. The basis for the proclamations was concern over environmental pollution. If these proclamations became effective, the organization's business would cease completely. In analyzing the dilemma, the manager noted that the following conditions pertained.

The manager's company had a strong *policy* of no collusion with competitors. In addition, company policies restricted the ways the manager could interact with the communities in which he did business. If he obeyed the policies to the letter, his only alternative was to shut down his business.

The manager was able to help the owners recognize the differences between the culture in which he operated and that of the parent company and was finally allowed to do some "experimenting" with relationships with competitors in the host country. The new strategy was for him to meet with his counterparts in competing organizations. Together they were able to find a constitutional lawyer who discovered some laws on the books of the country limiting the power of mayors to make proclamations in restraint of trade. Based on this information, the managers were able to get a restraining order, which gave them time to deal with the substance of the question of whether their products were in fact harmful to the environment. The manager recognized that of the two competing forces on him—to obey company policy and to cope with "local" demands—he *had* to respond primarily to the host country forces in order to deal with the substantive question.

In addition to a complex managerial choice of which way to move and with what consequences, the manager was faced with the need for a *recognition* that he had *no choice* about whether to respond to the pressure from the host country. In most of his previous managerial actions, his orientation had been to the company—the owners—and from that perspective he had choices about *how* to cope with the host country about a wide variety of situations. By analyzing the types of forces operating and becoming aware of his *lack* of choice about "whether," he was able to put his energy into creative strategies for *how* to effect the change.

Case Illustration 2: Misperception of the Choice of Whether to Make the Change

The management committee and chief executive of a large manufacturing company were confronted with the existance of an increasingly serious morale problem among middle management, including the threat of unionization of the professional and technical staff. The company was a large, decentralized organization with a number of profit centers, or business divisions, and a strong headquarters organization. In the past few years, the increasing influence of the trade unions, as well as progressive practices by the management, had often resulted in new, creative work designs, improved quality of working life at the shop floor, better compensation plans, and other changes. A great deal of energy had been put into improving relationships and redistributing earnings between owners and the workers, particularly those represented by the trade unions. A disproportionately low amount of energy had been expended on working with those salaried employees who were not so represented. These people had been most hurt by inflation and problems of the economy. Their morale was at an all-time low. Many professional and technical people, as well as junior management staff, felt that their only option was to organize and join trade unions.

Attempts to communicate this state of affairs to the organization's leadership had been stifled, either at the division management level or through central management's not "hearing" the messages. Personnel staff and others in touch with the state of the organization had sent several messages to the management group and to the chief executive reporting this state of affairs and outlining its potential implications. For a variety of reasons, the chief executive and many management-committee members chose to treat the entire condition as a minor upset which could be smoothed over.

The chief executive had personally visited several field operations and had received information that was (of course) quite inconsistent with what the staff people had been telling him. For him, the "objective" evidence of loyal and happy people who produced and thereby increased profitability and productivity was clear and overriding. He was unable to see or hear that there was real trouble afoot. Since he was approaching retirement, he did not want to initiate any major program that would upset the good performance results that had been achieved, even if a "morale" problem existed, which he doubted.

His retirement preceded by six months the assumption of office by his successor. At the time of the announcement of the new appointment, the new chief executive, who had been on the management committee, shared the retiring chief executive's attitudes toward the morale condition. He too did not see this as a major priority for top-management effort. However, he was very interested in getting a personal look at the general state of affairs and attitudes in the organization before he officially took office.

Helped by staff and consultants, he agreed to engage in a series of "listening meetings" in which he would visit each field operation and *listen* to the concerns of the people at various levels. The membership of the groups that he "listened to" was developed by a formula involving lateral representation at several levels as well as samples from different levels meeting in a "diagonal slice" group. In addition to division managers, the levels included middle managers, professional and technical staff, administrative and support people, shop stewards, shop workers, new employees, etc.; the "diagonal slice" group was fully representative of the total field organization. During these visits, the new CEO became acutely aware of the true state of affairs, and he became deeply concerned.

After completing his visits, he convened his top-management group and announced to his colleagues that he would be spending 50 percent of his personal time on this issue. He would become the "project manager" in order to get the condition changed. He instituted a series of monthly meetings with operating managers at various levels, so that he could personally and continually sense the state of affairs. He recommended strongly that heads of functions and businesses also conduct such activities. A senior field manager was assigned to make a study and recommend changes in both compensation and reward allocation to lower- and middle-management groups. He built in a feedback system through the line organization, which required his immediate subordinates to have up-to-date information on the attitudes of middle and junior management.

In this illustration, we can compare two strategies of managing the situation by the two chief executives who had the same set of forces but made two different *diagnoses*. For the first CEO, the forces for change within the organization were "communicated" through memos, reports, etc., by the staff to the organization management. This CEO diagnosed this as *staff* information which was not validated by his own experience, his *routine* visits to the field. His diagnosis of the *strength* of the forces from the field was almost totally erroneous. By contrast, the desire of the second chief executive to *find out* for himself what the situation really was enabled him to more accurately assess the strength of the forces. From his own field testing he recognized that the *de facto* situation was that he did *not* have a choice about *whether* to move to respond to these forces. His actions, his personal commitment of time and energy, and his follow-up in making sure that information kept flowing throughout the system resulted from a different *diagnosis* of the same set of facts. His strategy for managing the change and the situation was very different from that of his predecessor.

Case Illustration 3: Management Control Over Whether to Change—Misperception of Potency of Internal Forces

In the illustration above, forces both internal and external to the organization were operating. The first chief executive's response was primarily to the internal forces; he did not recognize the potency of the environment—the economic conditions on the people in the organization. In the following illustration the reverse is true; the external force was very clear and well understood. The chief executive recognized its clear potency and chose to respond to it actively, but was unaware of the potency of the internal forces resistant to carrying out those actions indicated by the external pressures.

This particular situation confronts many American organization leaders. Legislation and strong social pressure require organizations to conduct "affirmative action programs" and to hire, promote, and develop women and minority persons in particular proportions to the population, in the areas where the organization operates. Sanctions or punishments for not conforming to the legislation may result in an organization's not being able to do business or receive funds from any governmental source.

Any American organization today must have an affirmative action plan, with specific targets, numbers, and programs for achieving the goals. Organizations are subject to audit and can be cited for noncompliance, whereupon the various sanctions can be brought into effect. For the organization leadership, affirmative actions pose many, many problems: ability to recruit competent female and minority personnel, numbers of such personnel who can be hired without displacing white males, prejudices toward minorities and/or females, the time and effort needed to carry out such programs versus the requirements of the more results-related tasks, such as making and selling the goods.

Situation and Initial Strategy.   A chief executive had strong personal desires to take an activist position on affirmative action. He wanted the organization to have managers at all levels actively concerned about and motivated toward doing something to provide equal jobs and equal development for women and minorities. He had made his position very clear to his top-management group. He had personally gone out to the field and talked to plant managers and sales managers. He had made some video tapes in which he had defined his values and philosophy about the social responsibilities of the organization. He had provided staff-support personnel, including specialists in training and community organization, to assist line managers in carrying out an active program.

Diagnosis.   After a year of operating under this change strategy, it became very clear to him that the strategy was not working. A diagnosis of the reason revealed that although the CEO had the *official* authority and power as the leader of the organization, the *actual* power to change behavior was widely distributed. *He* did not hire women or blacks; plant managers and regional sales directors did. *His* attitudes toward both the legislation and the values underlying it were seen as much less relevant by these people than was the behavior of subordinate managers. They were responding to their perception of what behavior was rewarded or punished in the organization. The CEO's exhortations and personal biases did not affect them, particularly since many of his *immediate subordinates* did not share his more "liberal" stance. The real situation was a "compliance" strategy—do the minimum to stay out of jail or out of trouble. The chief executive's *desired* stance was an activist strategy—take a lead in social responsibility.

Revised Strategy and Action Steps.   On recognizing this actual response of middle managers—the compliance strategy—the CEO set about to change the organization's behavior. He appointed a young, bright, high-potential executive from one of the divisions to function from the chief executive's office as a *staff manager* for moving the affirmative action process along. From the top-management committee the CEO created a subcommittee headed by one of his senior colleagues and with another senior colleague as a member (both of these men were highly conservative in their views on this issue). They were supplemented by two other members of senior management. This group was set up as the affirmative action policy group. The staff manager was made executive secretary of this policy group. He developed an operations group to work in the field on specific programs to help line managers and also instituted and monitored procedures for implementing the policy decisions.

According to the procedures instituted, managers at all levels were required to submit on a quarterly basis a report on the status of their affirmative action activities, in addition to whatever business data they reported. This report included numbers of vacancies anticipated in the next three months, names of candidates for these vacancies and data on their sex and/or race, and specific plans for preparing these people for new jobs. (If names could not be identified, specific plans for getting names—"guesstimates"—of what the condition would be three months hence would be acceptable.) These reports were sent up the line, but unlike the business reports, which stopped two or three levels above the operations, these particular reports went up to the group vice-president of the business area. Copies of these reports were sent to the staff project manager, who tabulated them and submitted a summary to the chief executive officer at the end of each reporting period.

The strategy comprised:

1. Getting the commitment of the top leadership to do something about it;
2. Defining the reward system in such a way that a clear message went to the entire organization that affirmative action was an essential part of the work;
3. Setting up a system of control and information flow as opposed to expertise;
4. Using the power of the CEO to monitor the process rather than to advocate the process.

Here the executive manager did not initially recognize that his choice of control over whether or not to make the change he wanted was constrained by the behavior and attitudes of the people in the organization rather than by the demand of the legislation for the change. The original strategy assumed that the only demand that was out of his control was the demand to institute a plan.

WHAT NEEDS CHANGING?

We have been looking at who wants the change and what choices the manager has in responding to who wants it. We now turn to another side of the issue—*what* needs changing. This relates to our earlier discussion about taking the picture of the present. We have mentioned the need for determining the readiness and capability of different subsystems for the particular change. The next step is to find ways of increasing the organization's readiness and capability for the change. Some of the considerations are as follows.

1. If traditions, norms, and ways of work are locked in, the intervention will have to break people away from deeply held attitudes or behaviors to ready them to try something else. Some "unfreezing" intervention is indicated.

2. If the priorities or the goals of the organization are perceived so differently or are not shared, effective change can take place only if a goal-setting exercise or process is undertaken.

3. Structures probably need changing if the organization chart does not reflect the tasks to be done.

4. There may be a need for setting up some temporary systems and projects in order to get the change instituted if present structures are unable to do it.

5. Is new information or technical knowledge or skills required to achieve the change conditions? If so, some educational activities may be needed.

Case Illustration 1

Situation. A company that manufactured materials-handling equipment purchased a small electronics company that designed both the software and hardware of computer systems for running materials-handling vehicles. The technologies of both companies were complementary but very different. The new company was located several thousand miles away from the parent company, a third-generation, family-managed, single-technology organization located in a small town where it was the dominant employer. The new company was located in a large industrial park in California. Employees of the old company were conservative, old friends, and second generation. The employees of the acquired company were technical people, entrepreneurs, "modern electronics" scientists, and prima donnas.

Economic facts indicated that the two types of activities should ultimately be integrated. The executive management was faced with the choice of whether to (1) bring the new enterprise into the old physical setting, (2) operate them as two separate enterprises with a liaison group, or (3) work in a project organization. It was also faced with determining the management structure and information systems that needed to be developed. Should these two companies be two separate profit centers with general managers? Should the acquired organization be an arm of the technical function of the parent company?

Diagnosis. The top management of the parent company, in collaboration with top management of the acquired company, did an analysis along the lines indicated on p. 37. (1) In response to the question: Do the systems need "unfreezing"; are traditions and norms heavily locked in? the answer was yes for the old company and no for the new company. (2) Are the goals clear and universally shared? The answer was no. The goals of the personnel of the acquired company were invention, improved state of the art, entrepreneurial development, and get rich quick. The goals of key personnel in the old company were stability, moderate growth, values, etc. (3) Are the structures frozen in old ways or set to deal with ways which are no longer current? The answer was that they were not set in old ways, but were certainly inappropriate to the task of integrating the two technologies. (4) Do we need to set up a project system alongside the current operation? The answer to this was yes, probably several. It was agreed that certainly there was a need for a project organization to manage the integration of the two technologies on the same track. Further, it was decided that a project organization should probably be developed to look at resource allocation between the two organizations and that a project organization might be needed to manage the entire enterprise. (5) Is new information and/or technical knowledge and skills required to achieve the change condition available? The answer was yes, the knowledge is available and could be integrated. The view was that some of the technologies should remain separate because of the specialization, but other parts could be combined.

Strategy. From this diagnosis, top management developed the following strategy:

1. Do not try to physically integrate the two institutions or two groups in the first place.

2. Develop a project organization, with the technical leadership of both institutions collaborating on specific areas of technical and product integration.

3. Create a management structure for the project organization in which the head of the acquired company becomes its chief operating officer. Locate the *executive* function in a *group* composed of the chief operating officer, the vice-president of technical services, and the vice-president of operations from the parent company.

4. Work through the goals issue by having a significant group of the leadership of the acquired organization attend the parent company's management meetings.

This is a brief illustration of how the use of this set of questions determined managerial strategy.

Case Illustration 2

Situation. The leadership of a nursing college decided to make a major change in the way its curriculum was organized and nursing taught. The decision to make the change was based on the fact that nursing graduates' first jobs were more diverse than they had been in previous years. The current curriculum trained nurses to treat patients in hospitals, but did not place much emphasis on teaching them family care, dealing with ambulatory patients, working in community delivery settings, etc.

From a series of studies the faculty concluded that the best way to redress this imbalance was to change the *focus* of the curriculum from one of subject areas or disciplines, such as medical-surgical nursing, community nursing, etc., to one of type of patient care, e.g., "primary care" (continuing and preventive), "secondary care" (a more continuing back-up type of chronic care), and "tertiary care" (acute care in a hospital). It was felt that each of the three one-year curriculums should focus on *one* of these three types of care and that the various disciplines—medical, surgical, community nursing, etc.—should be slotted into these programs.

Although there had been general faculty agreement on the necessity for this change in order to meet the changing external demands, there were obviously all sorts of mixed and negative feelings from members of the faculty about loss of control, loss of status, loss of teaching quality, etc. The original strategy for managing the change had been for the dean to appoint a group of committees—mostly younger faculty who were advocates of the change—to do some planning of the new curriculum. Initial efforts had moved very slowly for a variety of reasons: reluctance of department heads to provide the time for junior faculty to work on the project, different degrees of commitment or motivation to work on the program, overwork and overload of activities to conduct the present curriculum.

Diagnosis.   The dean was rather frustrated with the progress of the change. An analysis of the situation elicited the following answers to the questions listed on p. 37. (1) Do various systems and groups need unfreezing and are traditions and norms operating? The answer was a strong yes. (2) Are goals so widely differentiated that some sort of goal-setting activity is necessary? The answer was that goals are generally shared, but means and priorities are widely differentiated. Some process for setting priorities would probably be required. (3) Are structures frozen in the old ways; is structural reorganization required? The answer was definitely yes. The new situation will be a different structure. (4) Do we need to set up a project system alongside the current operation in order to get the change instituted? There was a project system enforced—the curriculum-planning groups—but it was not working well. Diagnosis seemed to indicate the need for a whole new management system for the transition period, during which the old curriculum and the new curriculum would be conducted side by side. (5) Is new information of technical knowledge and skills required to achieve the change condition? Yes, the new curriculum implies team teaching, a process in which most people are inexperienced—the integration of different types of content is a new approach to teaching. The field work involved in the new curriculum will be very different from the traditional hospital practice that existed in the past. New educational activities clearly need to be instituted.

In weighing these various factors, the dean and her advisers recognized that of the various conditions, an unfreezing intervention to make the entire faculty aware of the organizational issues would probably need to precede any other activity. There was a need for some sort of activity which would allow the entire faculty to participate in defining where the crunches would be, what kind of management would be necessary, etc.

Strategy.   The dean began by convening a one-day *workshop* for the entire faculty. Outside experts from a nearby management school presented to the group an overview of the process of organizational change, some of the inherent problems in change, the need for and some methods for doing organizational diagnosis, some methods for analyzing the forces involved in an organization and for developing a strategy, some understanding of the difference between the old and new state of affairs, and the need for a management uniquely designed to govern the transition state.

A written case, which looked "strangely" like their own school, was presented for participants to "solve." Participants were divided into small working groups composed of older faculty, new faculty, department heads, and program heads, with each of the groups maximally heterogeneous. The groups were asked to analyze the "case school," develop a strategy for managing this transition to the new curriculum, and be prepared to advise the dean on how to manage the change. Then a representative from each subgroup reported its findings to a role-play dean (the real dean was in the room).

This simulated "confrontation" with the real situation made the entire faculty aware of the total situation and the problems involved. Everyone recognized that a management structure would need to be set up to manage this interim period.

The second major element in the strategy involved determining a *structure for managing the transition state.* Coordinators for each of the three curricula were selected from senior faculty by the dean, with the support of the functional department heads. Each one of them headed a different curriculum/development committee. Members of this committee were appointed by their department heads. The charter for each committee was to produce the curriculum. Membership did not necessarily imply that these same people would be teaching the courses.

The third part of the strategy was the development of a *coordinators' group*. A group headed by the curriculum coordinator for undergraduate programs managed the effort. This group reported directly to the dean and paralleled the existing hierarchy of department heads. Mechanisms were instituted for handling conflicts over priorities. Team-development activities were instituted for helping the new curriculum and teaching teams get to work effectively. Decision-making responsibilities were worked out through a process of meetings between department heads and curriculum heads, using a responsibility-charting process. The group of coordinators and the department heads periodically reviewed the priorities so that the goals became clear.

In review, the change strategy had several components. First was an educational activity to produce both technical knowledge and some "unfreezing" of attitudes. Second, the structures were reorganized to make them more congruent with the different types of tasks required during the transition. Third, a separate project-management group was formed to manage the transition. Fourth, activities were undertaken to clarify goals and goal priorities.

WHERE TO INTERVENE?

Having devised a strategy based on an analysis of the forces demanding change and the choices about whether to make the change and what needs changing, the manager is now faced with choices about where to start. Some of the subsystems of every organization that can be examined as alternative initial places to start are:

1. The top management or top of the system;

2. Management-ready systems—those groups or organizations known to be ready for the change;

3. "Hurting" systems—a special class of ready systems in which conditions have created acute discomfort in a previously unready system;

4. New teams or systems—systems without a history and whose tasks require a departure from old ways of operating;

5. Staffs—subsystems that will be required to assist in the implementation of later interventions;

6. Temporary project systems—those systems whose existence and tenure are problem-defined and whose task is to achieve a specific goal.

Looking back at our earlier cases, we can see that all of the choices made took into account this kind of question. For example, in the illustration of the materials-handling organization, early intervention was made at the top of the system through changing the governance; the creation of temporary systems was an early step in the nursing school case. The early interventions made with the management personnel and with the whole system can provide an effective alternative prior to working with specific systems, such as the ready group of advocates for the change or the new coordinator groups. Unfortunately, as in all of these, there is no "cookbook"—no sure-fire, predetermined solution. Our argument throughout is that if one asks questions systematically, one is likely to come up with better judgments and better choices.

CHOOSING INTERVENTION TECHNOLOGIES

In addition to examining where to start, another issue for analysis is choosing a technique or technology to use to move the process forward. Some possibilities, as we have already stated, are the use of an educational activity as an intervention, the redesign of a structure—a structural intervention, the creation of a new change management system, as in the affirmative action plan case.

A couple of general points can be made about the choice of initial interventions. One is to think through and identify the most likely possible early activities and their consequences. Some of these activities might be:

1. An across-the-board intervention, such as the faculty meeting in the nursing school;

2. A pilot project linked to the larger system, i.e., trying something out in one area as the first of a number of changes;

3. Experiments, which differ from pilot projects in that they may or may not be repeated to test different types of interventions to move a situation forward (for example, in the materials-handling case, a number of different types of groups were formed to try to find a model for communication between the two organizations);

4. An organizationwide confrontation meeting to bring together various parts of the organization to examine the current state of affairs;[1]

5. Educational interventions, as in the nursing school case;

6. Creating temporary management structures, e.g., the nursing school, the company with the affirmative action problem, and the materials-handling company.

One general point in making these choices is that it is important to remember that *it is most difficult for a stable organization to change itself, that is, for the regular structures of the organization to be the structures used to manage the change.* It is often necessary for temporary systems to be created to accomplish the change. In practically every illustration given above, this happened. Often, effective change effort requires novel solutions involving new ways of approaching problems. Existing mechanisms may be inappropriate in these situations.

We also strongly recommend that the choice of technology for managing the change be one of the later areas of selection by the management rather than an early decision. All too frequently, this is the first decision made by the management. We often hear from a management trying to change a situation: "What's needed here is a planning exercise" or "What's needed here is an MBO system" or "What's needed here is a management-training program." We are suggesting that those decisions are of relatively low effectiveness and somewhat high risk unless they are related to and grow out of the issues discussed earlier in this chapter.

---

1   R. Beckhard, "The Confrontation Meeting," *Harvard Business Review* **45**, 2 (March–April 1967): 149–155.

5
MANAGEMENT STRUCTURES
AND PROCESSES IN THE TRANSITION

In this chapter, we look at three major concepts. First, we consider various management mechanisms for the transition state—defining how the change will be managed. Next, we discuss developing a process or activity plan—specifying what actions must be taken in effecting the change. Finally, we note the importance of developing a commitment plan and strategy—identifying individuals whose commitment is critical and then specifying a strategy for gaining commitment to the change from those key actors.

MANAGEMENT MECHANISMS
FOR THE TRANSITION STATE

If the transition state is *unique or different* from either the prechange or the postchange condition, a separate structure and management congruent with the tasks and organization of resources required for this unique state are needed. For example, if one is replacing a book-keeping system with a computer-based electronic data-processing system, there are three sets of conditions: (1) those that existed before the change, (2) the condition that will exist when everything is on the computer and working properly, and (3) an intermediate condition, one that will exist as the computer comes on line and is debugged and as jobs change and as people learn new ways of working.

This last condition—the transition—has people working in relationships different from both those they had in the past and those they will have in the future. The critical question confronting the executive manager is: How should this time of transition be managed? Should the person in charge of the hand-bookkeeping operation be in charge of the change in terms of allocating work, rewarding people, determining timetables for going on the electronic system, etc.? Should the person who will be in charge of the work in the new system be in charge during the transition period? Should both people be in charge? Or should their common supervisor be in charge?

There is no cut-and-dried answer. However, if the question is: What is the most appropriate management system and structure for effectively managing this ambiguous transition state of affairs so that it creates the least tension with the ongoing system and the most opportunity to facilitate and develop the new system? the likelihood that *appropriate* management structures for this "state" will be developed will be significantly increased. For example, if one were to look at a new curriculum design involving different responsibilities, allocations of resources, assignments of teachers, etc., and to ask this question, there would probably be a time during which the old curriculum is being taught in the old configuration and the early parts of the new curriculum are being brought into the program. Again, a critical question facing the manager in this case is who should be managing the change—the heads of the old departments who managed and controlled the old curriculum, the program directors for the new curriculum, a special project manager, or the dean.

Some considerations in determining the particular management structure are finding someone who:

1. Can have the clout to mobilize the resources necessary to keep the change moving. Usually in such a change situation, one is competing for resources with others who have ongoing work to do.

2. Can have the respect of the existing operating leadership and the change advocates. A great deal of wisdom, objectivity, and linkage may be needed in order to make the balancing decisions, e.g., how much resource to put into the new activity and at what pace.

3. Has effective interpersonal skills. A great deal of the leadership at this time requires persuasion rather than force or formal power.

Depending on the nature of the change and the anticipated problems, different types of resources and mechanisms are appropriate to management of the transition. However, whatever the choice of transition management structure and personnel involved, making and communicating the explicit management decisions about management structure make a significant difference in the effectiveness of the transition. The following is a list of alternative structures for managing this state:

1. *The chief executive becomes the project manager.*   The *head person* takes responsibility for coordinating the change effort. For example, in the development of a new plant or a major change in a plant, the plant manager may personally function as project manager for the change; if this requires considerable energy, the day-to-day operations of the "present" may be delegated to others on the CEO's staff.

2. *A project manager.*   The executive manager may give either a staff person or a line person a temporary assignment. Here, the project manager functions from the executive manager's office and has the power of the executive office to manage the change. This alternative is very similar to that of a product manager in a technical organization. The product manager is a program integrator charged with the responsibility of getting the job done, but having to do so with resources whose "homerooms" are in other parts of the organization.

3. *The hierarchy.*   The change transition management is given as a separate or additional piece of work to the people who manage the operations. These individuals are thus "job-enriched" and have explicit responsibilities different from their usual operating responsibilities. An example is a management committee functioning as a new-products committee. As the organization moves from a functional to a matrix structure in order to improve interdepartmental integration and coordination for new-product development, the heads of technology, marketing, manufacturing, and newly assigned product managers would hold monthly meetings to make companywide decisions about new-product possibilities. For the functional heads, this type of activity would differ from their usual responsibilities.

4. *Representatives of constituencies.*   Here, the change management structure is a group that represents the major constituencies

involved in the change. For example, a new system of employee-management work relationships might be managed by a group representing both employees and managers. If one is moving toward more participation and democracy in working conditions, one might want representatives from blue-collar workers, technical and administrative junior management, senior management, and top management to monitor, oversee, and manage the change.

5. *"Natural" leaders.* Sometimes the executive manager selects a group whose members have the confidence and trust of large numbers of their colleagues, even though they may not be official representatives. For example, in a medical school the change would probably be facilitated if the chairman of medicine and the chairman of surgery and perhaps one or two others were to be involved and committed; then other departments and suborganizations would also become committed. Certain people in most organizations can "deliver a constituency."

6. *A diagonal slice throughout the organization.* This alternative is employed when there is a felt need to get continuing input from many different levels, cultures, and functions within the organization. The diagonal-slice mode involves getting a *representative* sample of the various functions, locations, and levels as opposed to getting *formal representatives of groups.*

7. *The "kitchen cabinet."* This American expression refers to those colleagues (or sometimes cronies) with whom the executive manager consults on an informal basis, but who in fact have high influence on both the executive manager and the organization. When the executive manager wishes to maintain direct control over the change and desires objective and candid input from others in the organization, yet is concerned that line management may have vested interest in various options and distort their input, the kitchen-cabinet alternative may be the appropriate mode. Most chief executives have two or three internal colleagues whom they trust and consult in this manner.

To summarize, we are saying that the executive manager should (1) define the transition state as a set of conditions separate from either the present state or the changed state; (2) determine what type of governance or management would be most effective; (3) set up such a management structure and system; and (4) communicate the existence of this structure or system to all relevant parties. The transition is facilitated in most cases by having a management system for the transition state that is separate, or at least *uniquely identified*, from either the present state of operations or the future state of affairs.

Case Illustration 1

In a large hospital, patient care was coordinated by interns who had the responsibility for a number of patients physically located in a number of different areas of the hospital. But the interns and residents in the medical ward felt strongly that patient care could be improved if more coordination of the care of individual patients were put in the hands of the nurse who was physically located in a specific geographical area with a specific number of patient beds. It was not proposed that nurses take over doctors' technical responsibility, only that the *coordination* of care could be better handled by the people who were in physical proximity to the patients. The residents also suggested that perhaps wherever possible, patients assigned to any one intern should be located close together in the hospital.

This proposal for a change in patient-care coordination went up through the normal administrative channels. The chief of medicine, to whom the residents reported, approved an experiment. The director of nursing, to whom the nurses reported, gave tacit approval. The hospital director was notified of the experiment and gave his blessing. The residents who were pushing for this change represented a minority of all the residents in the medical service. The chief of medicine assigned responsibility for the management of the transition to those interns and residents who wished to participate in this experiment and move toward this change. The experiment was approved by the hierarchy, but the transition management was in the hands of the advocates.

When the change was initiated, the residents found that there was terrific resistance throughout the hospital. Orderlies would not do the bed moving needed to put all of an intern's patients in the same geographical areas; instead, the young doctors moved beds, and this caused general chaos throughout the hospital—in the patient-reception area, the telephone department, the billing department, etc. Administrative people threatened to strike, and other residents joined in the general resistance to this kind of disruption. Many staff saw the change as negatively affecting patient care. The hospital director had to step in and renew his support of the experiment.

Since residents rotated on a monthly basis, a new group for the medical ward immediately went back to the old system. The experiment itself was seen by doctors, nurses, social workers, and particularly patients as very successful in terms of patient care and patient satisfaction. The disruption caused by the differential work patterns, however, was more than the system could handle, so at the first opportunity, it went back to its old condition. The problems might have been alleviated or overcome if a project management conducting the experiment from the chief of medicine's office could have insisted that this experiment be conducted twice or three times and could have served as a liaison with the affected parts of the hospital system, e.g., the administration and support services. However, there was no appropriate transition management to manage that transition state, and the experiment failed.

Case Illustration 2

A company was making a major change in the relationship between sales and manufacturing and in the control of the manufacturing scheduling, prioritizing, etc. The company was part of a multiplant organization making products for several different business areas. Its current-state system was something like a job shop. The various product groups submitted their own and the market's requirements for the product to the manufacturing management, who then used a formula to allocate how much of what product would be produced in what plant during the following work period. The practice had resulted in skewed inventories, delays in delivery, and a number of other dysfunctional conditions. The general manager of the operation decided that it was necessary to create a distribution department—a new management structure which would take the market demands, determine the requirements necessary to meet those demands, put those into scheduling requirements for plants in different parts of the country so as to optimize distribution of the products, and give this information to manufacturing management for production of the product.

The original structure managing the transition was to add this new department and department head—the distribution department—to the general manager's staff. The change was explained to every body, and the various functional heads were asked to work out the implementation. After a month or so it became apparent that the change had produced increased confusion because of new reporting lines (warehouses now reported to distribution rather than to plant management), new roles, changes in territory and "turf," etc. The general manager, sensing that the three functional heads would be unable to work together to operate the changed condition, created a new management mechanism, with himself as chairman of a committee composed of the head of manufacturing, the head of distribution, the person who would be coordinating field operations in the warehouses, the production scheduling czar for manufacturing, and a marketing analyst. This group became the "general management" of the change. This combination of people and the clout of the general manager's office worked to ensure the success of the change effort.

DEVELOPING AN ACTIVITY OR "PROCESS" PLAN

In addition to determining appropriate transition management structures, a "process" or activity plan for the change must also be planned. We are purposely using the jargon word "process" to highlight the fact that the *process* of change needs conscious management, just as any technical process does. Once the desired change objectives have been clarified and the present state of affairs made clear, an explicit plan specifying activities to be undertaken and critical incidents or events that must occur to get from here to there must be made. For example, the process plan for a major structural change would incorporate a timetable of events, e.g., when first moves will take place, when meetings will be held to clarify new roles, what information will be communicated to whom on what day, when the new structure will start to operate, etc.

In essence, the process plan is the roadmap for the change effort. An effective process plan has the following characteristics:

1. It is *purposeful*—the activities are clearly linked to the change goals and priorities;

2. It is *task-specific*—the types of activities involved are clearly identified rather than broadly generalized;

3. It is *integrated*—the discrete activities are linked;

4. It is *temporal*—it is time-sequenced;

5. It is *adaptable*—there are contingency plans and ways of adapting to unexpected forces;

6. It is *agreed to* by the top of the organization;

7. It is *cost-effective* in terms of the investment of both time and people.

Some precautions, however, are necessary in the development of an effective process plan. As with any other goal-setting process, a plan that is not specific and reviewable becomes simply a set of desired objectives rather than a requirement to achieve a certain activity. Frequently, the organization leadership assigns people to do the activities necessary to make the change—introduce the new procedure, develop the new technology, etc.—and treats these activities as enrichment or additions to present work. Since these additions or enrichments do not entail explicit rewards or punishments, they are not treated the same way that the operating work is; these efforts are regarded as extra activities rather than as fundamental work. Since the transition activities go unrewarded, people's energy will be directed to the area where the goodies come from. Therefore, management should be relatively explicit about seeing work on transitions and on change as part of the primary work of the people concerned, for which compensation and other rewards are allocated.

We will not pursue the obvious fact that a planned activity program tends to be better than an unplanned one. In managing complex change, most organizations do have specific plans for allocating resources and time; they do have critical or target points. Suffice it to emphasize that this systematic planning process is a necessary condition for optimum management of the transition.

DEVELOPING A COMMITMENT PLAN

Recent experience in organizational change has shown that in addition to developing the plan for carrying out the change, the planners must determine who in the organization *must* be committed to the change and to carrying it out if the change is actually to take place. Traditionally, managements consider this from a political stance, saying that they "have got to get a few people on board," "get the chief executive's approval," "have the agreement of the union leadership," or "have the majority of the engineers going along." We are suggesting here that in addition to the intuitive political judgment about "who needs to be committed," there is, and should be, a systematic analysis of the system to determine those subsystems, individuals, and groups, whose commitment to the idea, to providing resources (money and time), and to carrying out and persevering with the new process is necessary. Membership in these groups may vary.

Experience indicates strongly that in any complex change process, there is a *critical* mass of people whose commitment is necessary to provide the energy for a change to occur. It is impossible to quantify the number of people or the roles necessary to make the critical difference. For example, Ralph Nader and a few lawyers became a critical mass in affecting business enterprises and their practices.

One can, however, analyze the organization's systems that are affected by and affect the change and make a judgment about what a critical mass is for the particular change effort. We can define a "critical mass" as those individuals or groups whose active support will *ensure* that the change will take place. Their number may be small, but it is the critical number.

To give one illustration, a chief executive of a large, complex organization was very aware of the need for closer contact between the top-management committee and the division managements. When people got into the corporate headquarters and joined the management group there, they tended to become insulated and to some degree isolated from the operating divisions and the field. This was good in terms of autonomy and decentralized control of activities, but bad in terms of adequate information about people's attitudes toward their working conditions, etc. The company's management had been surprised by an attempt to organize junior middle management. The chief executive officer had made an extended "sensing trip" throughout the system. He had listened to people at all levels and ranks talk about their conditions. He had talked to his colleagues on the management committee, but not much behavior had changed. In diagnosing the desired change as a situation entailing a different set of relationships between members on the central management board and the general managers of divisions, he realized that the critical mass was four or five of the twelve members of his management committee. Those four or five had been with the company a long time, had been the norm setters, and would, if they changed their behavior, carry along their fellow management-committee members.

The CEO therefore developed a strategy for getting those four or five people to introduce new ways of behaving toward their field counterparts, the division general managers. He also knew that it was necessary to have some significant number, perhaps half, of the field general managers realize that they had to do something different; they needed to have better information about what was going on in their own divisions about such things as work conditions, and they needed to have a system for reporting this to the board or central management. For both the management committee and the division general managers, there was an identifiable number that made up a critical mass. Having identified the critical mass needed, the CEO wanted to make a specific plan for getting them "on board"—committed and involved.

A commitment plan is a strategy described by a series of action steps devised to secure the support of those subsystems which are vital to the change effort. The steps in developing a commitment plan are as follows:

1. Identify target individuals or groups whose commitment is needed;

2. Define the "critical mass" needed to ensure the effectiveness of the change;

3. Develop a plan for getting the commitment from the critical mass;

4. Develop a monitoring system to assess the progress.

Various alternatives can be used to get commitment of target individuals or groups identified as the critical mass.

1. *Problem-finding activities.* Oftentimes significant parts of the system are not aware that there is a problem. Thus by trying to clarify and identify a problem or a need, one sometimes gets the commitment of significant numbers of people. In the case illustrated above, the leadership of the organization—the management committee—got on board only after being threatened with the unionization issue and becoming aware that a problem existed.

2. *Educational activities.*   Sometimes the use of a training course or educational event will provide the kind of awareness and commitment which legislation or policy statements or directives cannot accomplish. For example, in Chapter 4 we said that the nursing school was changing from a discipline-based curriculum to a program- or utility-based curriculum. The school had been organized in functional departments (disciplines). In the new system, it would be necessary to organize around programs, such as a masters program or a doctoral program. The people who were assigned by the dean to manage the change were the young and assertive faculty who really wanted the new system. The faculty was organized into departments based on disciplines, and the leadership of those departments (the chairmen of the departments) tended to be the traditional discipline-oriented faculty.

When the change was started, the young people in charge of the programs found themselves confronting the experience and the clout of the discipline department heads. The rate of change and commitment of change was really controlled by the old power structure. An educational activity was mounted; after some description of the change process by the outside consultants, the entire faculty was broken into small groups to work a case and come up with a recommendation to "the dean" about how to manage the change. The real dean was in the room, but the representatives of each of these work groups had to publicly make some recommendations to a role-acting dean. The process of forced collaboration and forced diagnosis in an educational setting, which members of the old guard were willing to attend because it was not directly threatening the curriculum, produced a general awareness of what would be involved if the change were to take place. This process clarified the need for a powerful change management system. The plan developed provided for three coordinators for the three different programs, who reported directly to the dean instead of to discipline heads and who had the power and backing of the dean's office. The points at issue—the crunches that would come along during the change—were identified during this educational activity, and mechanisms were set up for managing them.

3. *Treating "hurting" systems.*   One way of moving the process forward is to begin work with those subsystems which are "hurting." Change is more likely to occur, and the "critical mass" is more likely to develop under this condition.

4. *Changing the rewards.*   In one large company, five profit centers sold different kinds of foods in a supermarket. The centers were grouped together because of the similarity of their marketing, even though each was an individual business and profit center. The group vice-president wanted the general managers of the various businesses to function as a "team" in thinking about future business strategy and priorities, in addition to their independent functioning in operating their businesses. Every Monday morning he convened them as a planning organization. The meetings were a disaster; people came late and left early, secretaries interrupted with "important messages," members found excuses for being out of town, etc. The group vice-president was pretty upset about this behavior and expressed it rather forcefully, but to no avail.

The company had a generous annual bonus system, and the group vice-president had the discretion about how it was to be distributed to his immediate subordinates. Shortly before one bonus period, he called his subordinates together and announced the criteria for the amount of the next bonus. Sixty percent would be based on the sales and profits of their own entities, 25 percent would be based on his subjective judgment of their contribution to the planning process, and 15 percent would be his opinion of the effectiveness of their people-development programs. The next meeting of the planning group was a totally different event from previous meetings.

5. *Functioning as a role model.*   Changed behavior by the leader is sometimes required in order to get changed behavior by others. In one large company, the chief executive officer was anxious to have better information than he was getting from his subordinates. He started a monthly series of "deep sensing" meetings with a sample of people from different suborganizations. He also let it be known that he thought this was a good process.

It did not take very long before these subordinates and division managers were also holding sensing meetings in their organizations. Although the subject had been brought up frequently before this, the activity that really facilitated the change was the chief executive's personal behavior.

6. *Forced-collaboration mechanisms.*   In order to get commitment, it is sometimes necessary to require people to work together and to take on certain managerial roles. In one company, more integrated management of affirmative action, manpower planning, and health

and safety was needed. Committees headed by members of the management committee were appointed by the CEO to manage these programs, which previously had been managed by specialists or staffs, and not enough had been accomplished. By putting people in charge who were the top management of the organization and who had to report to their colleagues and had to bring together any interested parts of the organization, the desired results were achieved and behavior was changed, even though some attitudes remained unchanged. For example, the people on the management committee who were in charge of the affirmative action program for the company tended to be those least sympathetic to the hiring of minorities and women into responsible positions. By having this assignment and being "forced" to manage the change, a critical mass was created that ensured the change.

The process of selecting a mechanism to involve those whose commitment is essential can be helped by analyzing the forces pro and con toward the change in both people and subsystems. A good principle to keep in mind is that if one can find an activity that loosens up the organization or unfreezes frozen attitudes, one may be alleviating the process of creating those conditions necessary for incurring a change of attitude, an increase in energy, and a greater commitment. The result is that less energy will be required than if one were to force the change on those who are resistent to it.

SUMMARY

The transition state, during which change takes place, is a unique set of conditions. It extends over time in large system change, and it requires separate management and governance structure. These structures may or may not be the same as those used for managing current future operations.

A systematic plan—with timetables, intermediate goals, and monitoring systems for designing the activities that need to occur in order to get the change introduced—is a helpful and perhaps necessary process if one wishes to minimize the confusion caused by the change. Perhaps even more important than the plan for the activities which will occur during the transition is a plan for defining whose commitment is prerequisite for the change to occur, developing a strategy for getting that commitment, and selecting specific activities to get commitment rather than the change itself.

6
INTERVENTION TECHNOLOGIES

In this chapter, we will look at three common problems in organization change and focus on three technologies for dealing with those problems. First, we will examine the issue of changes in the relationship between the organization to its environment and apply the technology of open-systems planning. Second, we will consider issues of changes in structure and apply some techniques and methods for matrix management. Third, we will look at changes in the way work is done, with particular emphasis on the problems of organizational interfaces and the application of "responsibility charting" as a way of managing change in this area.

We will try in each case to reexamine briefly the conditions defining the need for this particular technology, the technology itself, and some applications to organizational situations. It is not our purpose here to provide a cookbook of recipes for change management; rather, we want to identify and explore in some detail some of the more recent significant innovations in technology which we feel have wide application to the problems of managing organizational improvement.

THE ORGANIZATION AND ITS
ENVIRONMENT: OPEN-SYSTEMS PLANNING

The strength and diversity of forces outside organizations making demands on organization executives ensure their inclusion as factors in decision making. The executive can no longer make decisions about what is best for any one constituency. Each task must balance the interests of owners, employees, the larger community, and the physical environment—to name just a few. Given this complexity, executive decision making can be helped considerably if the participants have a clear picture of the strengths of the several forces and have criteria for making judgments on how to respond to them.

Most organizational theorists have long postulated that one should think of the organization as an *open* system. That is, the organization exists in an environment; the boundaries around the organization are permeable; and its interaction with its environment is a significant force in determining how the organization functions and develops. If one accepts this concept, planning an effective change strategy requires: (1) mapping the environmental forces and demands; (2) having a clear picture of present and desired organizational responses to these demands; (3) having a program of prioritized activities that are responsive to these demands; and (4) having a system for assessing the impact of these demands on the organization's objectives and activities over time.

Open-Systems Planning

In recent years the emergence of the increasing constellation of demands from environments surrounding organizations has caused some organizational leaders to aggressively search for, develop, and experiment with specific processes for their systemwide planning.[1] One such institutional planning process is the seven-phase open-systems planning. We will briefly describe what each phase involves and how it is used. In brief, the steps are:

1. Determine the "core mission" of the organization;

2. Map the demand system;

3. Map the current response system;

4. Project the probable demand system, given no change in organization impact;

1   *See* F. E. Emery and E. L. Trist, "The Causal Texture of Organizational Environments," *Human Relations* **18** (1965): 21–32; C. Krone, "Open Systems Redesign," in J. D. Adams, ed., *Theory and Method in Organization Development: An Evolutionary Process* (Arlington, Va.: NTL Institute for Applied Behavioral Science, 1974).

5. Identify the desired state;

6. List activities necessary to achieve the desired state;

7. Define cost-effective options.

The entire process of open-systems planning might be called a diagnostic process of preplanning. Basically, it is a process of analyzing the situation, identifying the kind of social and technical environment necessary to effectively operate, and developing a strategy for getting there.

Step One: Core Mission.   An organization *mission* is different from organization *objectives.* An organization's *mission* is its *reason for being;* an organization's objectives are its goals, the states it wants to achieve. Organizational leaders tend to take the organization mission for granted. For example, business organizational leaders might say, "Our mission is to maximize profits for the shareholders"; directors of a medical school might say, "Our mission is to train doctors" or "Our mission is to do biomedical research, furthering knowledge and providing opportunities for doctors to be trained in the most advanced technology."

Based on the statements above, one could define the organizational *mission* of a business enterprise as: (1) to maximize return of investment to shareholders, (2) to optimize return on investment, (3) to survive, (4) to provide more useful products to society, and (5) to provide employment. Or, one could say that the *core mission* of the medical school is: (1) to do biomedical research, (2) to train doctors, and (3) to provide through its teaching hospitals the specialty care not available in other delivery settings.

In one sense, the organizational missions are all of these. The problem is that a *core* mission cannot be *equally all* of these; it must be only one. In a complex organization with a variety of *conflicting* demands for allocation of resources, programs or investment priorities, and distribution of profits or other "goodies," the executive management must make the often painful choice of which "mission" is number *one*—which one is the *core* mission. If the core mission is to *maximize* return to shareholders, that maximization defines and bounds many managerial plans and actions. If, on the other hand, the *core* mission is to provide employment, the implications for managerial strategy and actions are quite different.

In a simple organization, it does not matter very much to what degree one differentiates the various mission statements. For example, suppose that Alice Smith's hobby is to make ceramic pieces; her mission at this point is to make ceramic pieces for her own enjoyment. If, after a while, she starts to give away these objects to friends and a friend says, "Look, these are quite marketable. If you could make more of them, I think we could open a store to sell them, and you could have the fun of making them while getting some money as well. If you make them, I will market them." We now have the beginnings of a complex organization, and the mission becomes a little more clouded. Is the "core reason for being" to have fun, to make money, or what? If the store that originally ordered ten of these now orders a thousand, different kinds of machinery and production processes are required. What now becomes the mission and what implications grow out of the changed conditions? Alice now has to make significant *personal* choices; does she want to "go into business" or stay out of business and keep her hobby?

All sorts of operational decisions grow out of this prioritizing. Managers of economic enterprises are very familiar with the dilemma of the conflicting missions of growth and maximizing short-term profits. One cannot have it both ways, so all sorts of trade-offs must be made, based on some manager's or group of managers' personal judgment based on an analysis of which is the more important of the two mission statements. Similarly, in the medical school with the three missions, the way the school actually operates, the type of faculty recruited, budget allocations, the relationship of teaching to research, etc., are all functions of whether the *leadership* of the institution sees the *primary* mission as teaching doctors, conducting biomedical research and science, or delivering patient care.

One can look at schools or at economic organizations or governments around the world and see clear differences based on the leaders' definition of the core mission. The point is that although it may seem obvious or busy work, top management must invest the energy in being clear about and having consensus on priorities and the core mission.

Determining the core mission requires an analysis of the character of the markets—the owners', employers', and/or the consumers' needs for inputs or outputs from the organization. In the case examples later in the chapter, we describe how three different executive managements made these choices and the resultant managerial acts. Two points should be emphasized:

1. The operable decision about *core mission* is the one that the top management of the organization *believes* and *uses* to guide its priorities in goal setting, resource allocation, etc. It is always, in the final analysis, a personal judgment of one or a few key executives.

2. It is important—often crucial—that the key executive management of the organization have consensus about the mission. If they don't, their behavior can produce very confusing consequences, resulting in mixed commitment to organization *goal* priorities, which flow from the *mission* definition.

Step Two: Mapping the Demand System.   At any given time, there are a number of different groups, institutions, and organizations making demands on the organization's leaders. Executive management must sort these demands in terms of the organization's mission and goal priorities and in terms of whether they *must* meet the demands.

In putting these demands in perspective and in relationship to one another, it is helpful to make a map of the "demanding institutions or groups" and to identify *what* they are demanding. A technique called "environmental mapping" has been developed to facilitate this process. First, management develops a visual chart, listing all of the groups, institutions, or conditions (the jargon word is "domains") that are saying to the organization, "We want you to . . . !" Next, five to ten of the most relevant "domains" are selected, and a list of their specific demands is developed. For example, the trade unions might demand higher wages, salaries, and benefits for their members; young employees might want a different kind of socialization process and increased opportunities to move ahead faster; environmentalists might want the organization to invest significant sums of capital to reduce present pollution from its operations or plants; senior management might want a totally different basis of compensation and work organization; the government of a country may want the organization leaders to emphasize employment rather than profit; the board and the shareholders may demand an increased return on investment in the short run.

After mapping the demand system, the next step is to identify present organizational responses to these demands.

Step Three: Current Response System.   Now the organization's current response to *each* of the demands identified in the previous phase is specified. For example, given demands from the government, women and minorities employed in the company or organization, and citizens' groups for the organization to increase its affirmative action activity, the organization may respond from any one of a variety of *response patterns.* One is to "do as little as you can, just enough to stay out of jail." Another is to "do what the others do"—the average of the industry or community. A third is to take an active posture toward the demands, e.g., setting improvement targets and committing resources for training and recruitment activities aimed at achieving those targets. Most organizations give lip service to this response pattern, but their practice is quite different.

Whichever response is adopted, everyone at the top-management level must agree to it. The process of working toward consensus of response also provides opportunities for assessing the consequences of different responses. For example, an organization's decision to minimize its affirmative action response may lead to loss of government contracts, legal suits, or both. Therefore, this response pattern is a relatively uneconomic and "unsocial" one to maintain.

Step Four: Projected Demand System.   The next step in the process is for management to make a three- or four-year projection of the likely demands if the organization were to do nothing significant in response to the demands on it. For example, is consumerism likely to be stronger, weaker, or about the same three years from now? Is Ralph Nader's movement likely to have more, less, or the same impact on the organization's policies and practices as it does now? Laid against the current response system, this type of projection increases the clarity of likely consequences of the current response set and allows one to move to the next step.

Step Five: Desired State.   The next step is to define what one *would like* the conditions to be in three or four years. For example, leaders of a private enterprise might want the government to be giving more support to private industry through increased tax relief. They might also hope for their organization to be regarded as the most desirable place to work by significant numbers of the brightest college graduates. In short, the map of the desired state provides some relatively clear and specific goal statements and the basis for beginning to identify a set of actions and activities for moving toward a more desirable condition.

Step Six: Activity Planning.   Here, the process is to identify those types of activities, organizational forms, investments, projects, etc., that would be necessary to achieve the desired state.

Step Seven: Assessing Cost-Effectiveness.   This is an analysis of both the social and economic costs of the action alternatives identified in the previous step and leads into strategic planning.

Some Applications: Case Illustrations of Open-Systems Planning

Case 1: A New Manufacturing Plant.   A company making and selling a variety of consumer products was building a new plant designed to produce a very popular product for which manufacturing capacity needed to be increased. Each manufacturing plant of the parent company was a cost center, producing a product according to requirements from the profit-center marketing organizations. Orders to the plant and distribution were both controlled by the marketing organization.

This new plant was to produce "glup," using a technology already highly developed and in practice in other plants producing the same product. Raw material came in a powdered form into an assembly line from a warehouse, was poured into a big funnellike machine that mixed it with some other materials, and was produced as an output product, also in powdered form. Through a relatively highly automated process, this finished product was put in boxes or bottles, which were then packed, sealed, stacked, and prepared for shipment.

In other plants using this technology, the production line required five operators, as well as a maintenance person available to handle any mechanical problems with the equipment, as shutdowns were extremely costly. A foreman supervised the five operators and machine-maintenance person.

The new plant was to be built in a small midwestern town and would have a major impact on the community, providing significant employment and tax revenue. Based on previous experiments using open-systems concepts to open plants, management decided that this plant would be socially and technically designed from the outset. A task force composed of the plant manager, the engineers building the plant, behavioral science—oriented staff, operations research and information systems people, and significant group leaders from the plant was named a design team and given wide latitude to innovate.

First, the task force examined the *core* mission of the new plant. What is to be the nature of this plant? All similar plants in the company had as their core mission the producing of a high-quality, optimum-cost product as needed by the company. This design team said no, the core mission of the new plant is to be in the "glup" business. Therefore, rather than being a cost center producing a product, the new plant's linkages with the environment around it, including headquarters management, distribution, etc., would have to be very different. For example, under the old system, the inventories held by a plant could become very expensive, depending on the whims of the marketplace. Because the plant was not measured on that basis, however, it was possible to operate considerably under optimum effectiveness. In the new design, the plant management and the brand management together would be looking at how to optimize such things as inventories.

From this core mission, the design team looked at the demands on both the technology and the people—at the traditional demands of having as tight a work force as possible, five operators to a shift. The team looked at demands in the engineering area for having full-time technicians at each machine, demands on the system for having adequate control systems for ordering supplies and flow of work, and the present responses or operating procedures of other plants.

Next, the team defined an ideal state, based on the core mission; being in the "glup" business, the team members said they wanted to do everything to maximize return on investment, as well as to create a work environment that would ensure effective work and growth of the people. Examining the concept of five people to a shift, for example, the team discovered that having six people on the shift managing the total work environment might make more economic and social sense. Rather than simply having the number of workers absolutely needed, there would be slack resources so that replacements could be drawn whenever there were an illness or tardiness or other difficulty.

The design team looked at the way supplies came into the line and devised a method of materials flow control based on the shortest-distance-between-two-points concept. That is, the person in the position on the line where the materials were received would now also be responsible for making sure there was inventory, and that person would have a direct line to inventory distribution as well. This change eliminated the necessity of going through three levels of management.

The team also looked at the technology of breakdowns and found that it would be possible for the various lines to have fewer technicians; these few would be a pool available to work on a number of problems. Operators would learn some first-level maintenance, which previously had been done by the specialists.

Everyone was put on an annual wage, based on both function and knowledge. When the plant opened, everybody started as a technician IV, able to do three of the five jobs; as people learned other jobs, they were upgraded to technician III, II, etc., and ultimately reached the top grade. From the outset, all workers were treated as multitask workers able to cover several positions. Decisions as to who would cover which position on what shift were matters to be dealt with by the team.

In recruiting actual work staff, the company went to the community, which had a large population of unemployed blacks. The company officials talked with community leaders and offered employment to their people. The leaders indicated that the community would prefer more people to have work, even though it would not be full time. As a result, company employment was for larger numbers of people working shorter weeks.

The design committee was replaced by a plant manager's work team, which included people at all levels in the plant. The design of each aspect of both the work and the work environment was to be conducted and reviewed by those who were doing the work. This approach has been successful; for several years the plant's productivity has been about 20 percent higher than that of other plants in the same system producing the same product.

Case 2: The Midstate Medical Center.   A large medical school was faced with the common problem of making some crucial choices about the priorities of its activities and the allocation of its financial and human resources. The school was located in a village several hundred miles from the main university's hospital facilities. Instead, a small community hospital served as a training location for *some* medical students; many others had to do their field practice in larger hospitals elsewhere in the state.

Many of the school's faculty members were highly competent in both the basic sciences and the clinical practices, such as medicine and surgery. In times past, research grants had provided much of the funding for the basic sciences. Because the community was unable to provide much income through patient care, it would be necessary to increase both the number of hospital beds and, more significantly, the level of out-patient care. If such a program were undertaken and staff assigned, it would seriously affect the budget available for research and the hiring of scientific faculty.

The dean's dilemma in defining the medical school's direction was serious. Obviously, many of the faculty members wanted to maintain the research emphasis. The hospital administration wanted to increase the cost-effectiveness of patient care; the citizens in the community and significant members of the board of trustees wanted an increase in service to the community.

The dean convened a conference of key representatives of some of the constituencies: hospital director, key faculty representatives, university administrators, etc. Using an open-systems planning model, their first and most extensive activity was to work toward a consensus on the core mission of this particular school. After a great deal of discussion, debate, and conflict, they concluded, not too enthusiastically, that the core mission for this particular school needed to be the training of doctors for delivering care to the community. This would mean some changes in budget allocations, some probable loss of present faculty, and difficulties in recruiting distinguished new faculty.

Having made the core-mission decision, the conference members were then able to look at the domains making demands on the school administration, look at the present responses, and develop a strategy for different responses. In the process of working through the model, they found that they would be more able to maintain faculty excellence and research capability than they had previously thought possible. They did, however, move the major thrust of the medical center toward the improvement of delivery and training of doctors for primary, or direct, care. This effort has affected the recruitment of students and faculty. Today the quality of the school's faculty and research is average or above. The training and education the medical students receive at the school are considered first-class, and the school has significantly increased its community service, even though it has lost some faculty and a number of activities have had to be redesigned.

Case 3: The Western School of Medicine.   A large, distinguished western medical school used this same process, but arrived at the opposite conclusion. This school's decision was that its core mission was to maintain the quality of its biomedical research. The school wished to train doctors primarily for graduate activities in the leading edges of applied science and was less concerned about training the general practitioner and only minimally concerned with providing health care to the community in which it was located. In fact, there was a quite adequate physician distribution in the area surrounding the school.

Summary and Conclusion.   In summary, where there is complexity in an organization, there is likely to be conflict of priorities about not only goals, but also the nature of the organizational reason for existing. If it keeps in mind the social, ecological, and economic interdependency in the environment today, management will likely want to clarify the priorities of the organization's current mission. If the mission is separated from the goals and is defined first, goals and priorities can be set within a context of agreement about the nature of the organization.

Once this mission is agreed on, it is often desirable to start the planning process by looking at the demands of the environment on the enterprise, rather than the other way around. Once these demands have been identified and a "snapshot" of the present response system recorded, change managers can be much more confident, and probably more accurate as well, in developing strategic plans for moving the organization ahead. It is also possible to be more aware of the normal and accentuated resistance to change that is likely to exist in the turbulent times and to plan strategies for coping with that.

In all three of the cases presented, the working through and defining the core mission provided guidelines for setting the management systems, recruitment systems, priorities, and other necessary activities within the institution. The technology of open-systems planning can, we feel, be a useful methodology for working through the complex issues facing current organizations.

CHANGES IN ORGANIZATION STRUCTURE/MANAGING MATRICES

As task complexity increases and old organization forms become less and less adequate to effectively do the work, organization managers are faced with new pressures to design structures that fit the changing work pattern.

Structure Defined by Work—Form Follows Function

The recent increasing complexity of the environment and more sophisticated technology have caused many organizational theorists and organizational leaders to reexamine some of their basic assumptions about how to design organizational structure. Historically, structure has frequently been defined by reporting requirements and control needs rather than by considering the nature of the tasks. Let us look briefly at a different way of thinking about organizations.

What the organization does—its activity—is to *transform* raw materials or needs for service into products and services of some value to some portion of the environment. This *transformation* process is the *work* of the organization. For the work of the organization to be done, there must be adequate information flow between parts, that is, *communications*. There must be machinery for making *decisions* based on the best information available. There is in fact the need for some people and/or roles to control and monitor the behavior of other people and roles; therefore, there is a power structure. This authorized, or official, power structure is called the authority structure, and it is this "formal" authority structure that most organization charts reflect.

We are all familiar with the concept of hierarchy. Early organization structures were based on designs for the military and the Catholic Church; in both institutions real power and the authorized power are highly congruent. For example, a person who does not follow military rules may be court-martialed; one who does not play the game according to the rules of the Catholic Church may be excommunicated.

Controls are not nearly so absolute in today's private or public enterprises. Yet organizations continue to be designed according to an authority structure. We contend, however, that the organization structure should be designed on the basis of the *work requirements,* that all of the other processes—communications, decision making, etc.—are means by which the work gets done, whether well or poorly. Therefore, as a method of analysis, one should look at the different types of tasks and organize the people of the organization to optimize work on those tasks. It follows that one will have more than one structure if one has many kinds of tasks.

For example, in thinking about the task and its relationship to the environment, one might come up with the following kinds of descriptions: (1) a sales department in a business organization interfaces and relates to a dynamic market; and (2) a production department, on the other hand, relates to a relatively stable technical or production process. Then, if one were "casting the characters" for each of these types of tasks, one would probably recruit very different types of people. For the sales jobs, one would probably want high-energy, initiative-taking people who were free to travel; for the production jobs, one might prefer relatively stable, responsible, family-centered, unambitious people who enjoyed doing a job well, even though the job didn't change.

One might also organize the tasks of the sales and production departments very differently. The kind of supervision needed for a group of entrepreneurial salespeople is totally different from that needed for a group of production people working on the same machines in the same location day after day. The reward and compensation systems might also be (and often are) very different. It is common practice to pay salespeople on a commission basis, but virtually unheard of to do that in production, and it is rare that one even finds profit sharing. Despite these differences, however, many organizations use the same criteria for evaluating performance, doing career planning, and often even assigning work schedules.

A hotel provides a good illustration of a highly differentiated operation. A hotel is simultaneously a restaurant, an inn, a laundry, a catering business, etc. By looking at the tasks, one can organize the reception area on a shift basis and train people to do the same tasks regardless of shift; the tasks do not change. On the other hand, tasks in the banquet department change tremendously from time to time, as do the requirements for presence of people on the site. Therefore, it would be ridiculous to put the banquet captain on the same type of schedule as the reception people. The banquet person needs to be there when there is a banquet, which may last until two in the morning. He or she does not need to be there at nine in the morning in order to meet a shift requirement. Similarly, the maids may be needed in the morning to make beds and perhaps in the late afternoon to turn down beds for the evening, and this situation might demand yet another type of shift operation.

Organization Redesign—A Response to Increasing Complexity

In companion books in this series, Jay Galbraith (1973) and Davis and Lawrence (1977) have described different types of tasks.[2] Let us briefly summarize the types and bases of organization structure.

New organizations, simple organizations, and some complex organizations are basically organized along the lines of general classes of major technologies. Such organizations are known as *functional* organizations. It is common to see in a business enterprise the structure built around major functions such as sales, production, finance, and research. The functions in a medical school are likely to be discipline-based, such as medicine, surgery, biochemistry, etc.

As tasks become more complex, it is often necessary to create a mission-based organization, e.g., the 747 airplane program, the foods division of a consumer-products company, the primary-care unit of a medical center, the masters degree program in a university. Organizations tend to move from their basic functional structure to a program, project, or mission structure when the types of products and services produced are differentiated enough to warrant setting up either a program or a profit center for each area. As organizations grow further and each of the profit centers requires the technologies represented in each of the other organization's basic function areas, such as accounting, personnel, or engineering, the headquarters organization will eventually become a holding company for a group of separate entities, each possessing all of the functions. For many organizations, achievement of this state is economically and often functionally impossible.

---

2   J. Galbraith, *Designing Complex Organizations* (Reading, Mass.: Addison-Wesley, 1973); Stanley M. Davis and Paul R. Lawrence. *Matrix Organizations* (Reading, Mass.: Addison-Wesley, 1977).

It is at this point that organization leaders tend to turn to a *matrix* organization, one in which a particular function or technology, as represented by a person or group, might be assigned to or live in one or more program organization. For example, a specialist with a background in package-design research who is assigned to a product organization, e.g., producing and selling toothpaste, is "matrixed," in the sense that she or he simultaneously reports to both the product manager and the packaging-research manager.

Issues in Matrix Management.   When a person or group reports to both a program and a technology area—a matrix structure—there are some inevitable and predictable consequences. Who makes what decisions? Who evaluates the performance of the person in the matrix? Who primarily influences career development and outcomes? How is conflict within the matrix structure resolved?

Allen and his colleagues have done studies of matrix structure and its effects on individual behavior.[3] These studies show, among other things, that three critical variables affect how a person responds to the matrix:

1. *Physical location/physical proximity*—where the matrixed person's desk or office is located tends to define the individual's primary loyalty, commitment, and orientation;

2. *Who appraises performance;*

3. *Who assigns work*—if most of the work is assigned from one end of the matrix, the individual's orientation and identity tends to be in that direction.

Our own observations and experiences have shown that the existence of a matrix has the following human consequences:

1. Requirements for simultaneous loyalties to the technology and the mission result in increased ambiguity not only for the individual matrixed, but also for those to whom the matrixed person reports. This ambiguity demands tolerance from all involved.

---

3   *See* T. J. Allen, "Communication Networks in R&D Laboratories," *R&D Management* **1**, 1 (1970): 14–21; T. J. Allen and I. Cohen, "Information Flow in Research and Development Laboratories," *Administrative Science Quarterly* **14**, 1 (March 1969):12–19.

2. Conflict is inherent in the matrix situation. Conflict arises over time allocation of the matrixed resource, performance-appraisal criteria, etc.

3. There is a need for increased communication within the system concerning work assignments, priorities, performance review, career planning, etc.

4. There is a need for decentralization of authority for priority setting and work planning. If the problem of matrix management is viewed as one of optimally allocating a scarce resource and the solution lies with the place of best information, clearly it is the matrixed person, not the boss, who possesses the most complete information needed to deal with the situation.

5. There is a period, probably lengthy, of adjustment and readjustment—of *learning*—during which the organization develops its capability and mechanisms to effectively work in the matrix structure. In her recent study of matrix-structured systems, Kay Whitmore (1975) concluded:

> The commitment to introduce a matrix structure must allow for an extended period of time for implementation, working out the initial problems, and learning to use the structure to meet the organization's needs. The companies in this study that had recently introduced a matrix organization had spent six months putting the new structure in place. This was then followed by a period of over one year in which small adjustments were required to solve unexpected problems.
>
> A major conclusion . . . is that there is a learning curve effect which may take longer than two years to begin leveling out. [The data indicate] . . . that individuals working within a matrix continue to learn how to operate within the structure, to improve their ability to make the system work, and to become more satisfied with this structural form through the first two or more years.[4]

---

4   K. R. Whitmore, "Matrix Organizations in Conventional Manufacturing-Marketing Companies," Master's thesis (Cambridge, Mass.: Sloan School of Management, M.I.T., June 1975), p. 69.

It is extremely important that the matrix managers develop specific methods for resolving certain issues. For example, in the illustration above of a package-design researcher located in a product-management organization, the managers of the two organizations and the incumbent worked out a *modus operandi*. For improvements of present packages, customer service, modifications and design for the next years, etc., the person is a member of a product team, calling on the technology group (package research) for resources and technical guidance. On matters of long-range product development, testing of new technologies, and the like, the person is a member of the technology unit, calling on the product unit for such resources as field testing and customer reactions.

By defining these kinds of classes of tasks and roles for all concerned, but particularly for the person who is matrixed, the ambiguity is considerably reduced, although not eliminated. We are suggesting that the managers of the poles of the matrix *together* perform a task analysis, preferably with the role incumbents, of the classes of tasks to be performed and specify and clarify the role relationships of the person who is matrixed and those to whom he or she will be reporting, for each class of task. Conscious effort toward this activity can significantly reduce ambiguity and unnecessary conflict.

Some Illustrations: Organization Redesign

1. In a community health center delivering stand-up care to a population of 40,000 people in an urban ghetto neighborhood, the structural organization was exactly like the hospital of which the health center was a part. It was basically a functional organization. Health care was delivered by teams composed of pediatricians, internists, nurses, and family-health workers. The internists reported to the chief internist; pediatricians, to the chief pediatrician; and the nurses, to the chief nurse. Each team delivered care to a specific geographic segment of the neighborhood and made all decisions about patient care; reporting lines, however, were to the functional, technology, or discipline areas. Much efficiency was lost, much grumbling existed, and a great deal of effort was spent in discussing how to get along in the system.

An organization redesign was developed in which the heads of the various disciplines—e.g., medicine, pediatrics—were defined as the health-services unit and were moved to a staff rather than a line responsibility. Their tasks included developing new protocols for treatment, providing quality control over the care delivered by the teams, and professional development of their colleagues. The delivery of care tasks was entrusted to the teams, and a new role—that of unit manager—was created. The unit manager was made responsible for providing the linkage between the delivery team and the types of resources the team needed, such as medical records, medical administration, and financial accounting. This redesign, although very painful and nontraditional, freed the teams and enabled them to focus on managing the tasks which they should manage and ultimately freed the professional leadership to focus its energy on professional matters rather than day-to-day operations.

2. A product-development organization of a large corporation was organized along functional (discipline) lines. Their connections with the marketplace were through the marketing organization and the top of the product-development organization. New products were slow in coming, intelligence about market needs was limited in the technical area, and acceptance of the belief in a close relationship between new products and organization survival was pretty much limited to the marketing and general management areas. In conjunction with marketing and product-development senior management, top management of the firm decided that it was necessary to get product development more integrally involved and proactive in its posture toward new-product development.

It was decided to redesign the product-development organization, creating product-technical managers, each of whom had primarily a product-orientation, but all of whose resources were technical people. The product-technical manager was assigned resources from the various disciplines, which now made up the product team. As these resources were still connected to their technology or discipline base, they were in fact matrixed. It was therefore necessary, as indicated above, for the managers of both the product and the technology groups to develop a *modus operandi* for the management of the matrix.

Summary

In this section, we are saying that as tasks become more complex and differentiated, it is often necessary to reexamine the structural configuration of the organization and to develop structures more closely related to the tasks to be performed. Form should follow function. That is, the tasks or activities (functions) to be performed first need to be examined and prioritized; then an appropriate structure (form) that facilitates the accomplishment of those tasks needs to be developed.

Organizations evolve from functional structures to mission or program-structures, and sometimes, necessarily, to matrix structures. Where matrix structures exist, it should be recognized that there are likely to be conditions of increased ambiguity, multiple loyalty, confusion over decision making, and communications difficulties. Therefore, management of a matrix requires explicit methods and programs for defining the types of tasks, role responsibilities for the different tasks, and feedback systems for ensuring continued communication and information.

PLANNING PROCEDURES/MANAGING
INTERFACES/CHARTING RESPONSIBILITY

From new structures, multiple roles, and new reporting relationships emerge problems of job definitions, reporting lines, accountability, and performance review. In managing a change effort in a large system, the point of pressure for change will probably occur at some organizational interface. Significant changes occur when: (1) the task relationships between, say, market research and market development are reorganized; (2) it is necessary to superimpose programs on top of functional organizations; or (3) there are mergers of different organizations with different backgrounds or cultures. Such reorganizations tend to have some characteristics of a matrix organization —increased ambiguity, role confusion, problems with decision making, and communications problems.

The typical ways of resolving these dilemmas are to:

1. Try to get clearer job descriptions of each job or position involved;

2. Use a mediating mode, e.g., upper management defines the responsibilities of the various roles;

3. Utilize intergroup development activities designed to clarify responsibilities, authority, and rewards.

Most of these efforts do not succeed too well, however, because they are focused on improving the decision making *or* the communications *or* the power. They are not focused directly on *optimizing work,* although they may appear to.

Responsibility Charting

In recent years a new technique has emerged which does focus on allocating work responsibilities; this technique is called *responsibility charting*. The first step is to construct a grid; the types of decisions and classes of actions that need to be taken in the total area of work under discussion are listed along the left-hand side of the grid, and the actors who might play some part in decision making on those issues are identified across the top of the grid (see Fig. 6.1).

The process, then, is one of assigning a behavior to each of the actors opposite each of the issues. There are four classes of behavior:

1. *Responsibility (R)*—the responsibility to initiate action to ensure that the decision is carried out. For example, it would be a department head's responsibility (R) to initiate the departmental budget.

2. *Approval required, or the right to veto (A–V)*—the particular item must be reviewed by the particular role occupant, and this person has the option of either vetoing or approving it.

3. *Support (S)*—providing logistical support and resources for the particular item.

4. *Inform (I)—must be* informed and, by inference, cannot influence.

Each item is considered and responsibility (R) assigned. A very important aspect of the technique is that there can be only *one* R on any one horizontal line. Therefore, a consensus must be reached or an authoritarian decision made on who has the responsibility. If the group is unable to agree about where the R should go, there are three options:

1. Break the problem out—always the most desirable alternative. For example, the R for a large capital expenditure might be different from the R for a small capital expenditure.

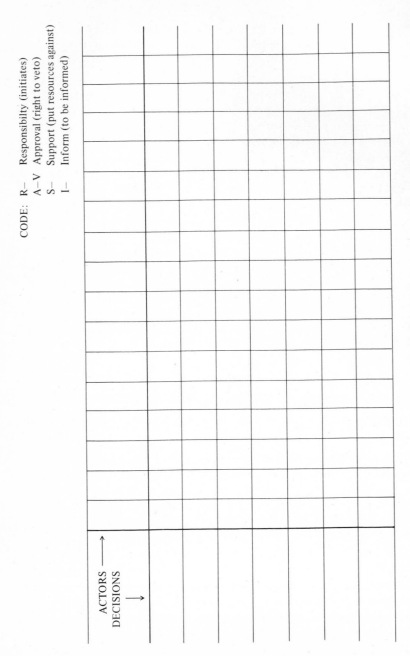

CODE: R–   Responsibilty (initiates)
A–V Approval (right to veto)
S–   Support (put resources against)
I–   Inform (to be informed)

ACTORS ——→
DECISIONS →

Fig. 6.1 Responsibility chart.

2. Move the R up one level in the organization hierarchy. For example, if the marketing manager and production manager cannot agree which one of them should have the R for defining monthly production targets, move the R up to their boss, the division general manager.

3. Move the *decision about assigning the* R up one level. In the previous example, the division general manager would assign the R for setting production targets rather than define the targets themselves.

Once the R has been assigned, the next step is to take a new item and assign a behavior for the various actors. In addition to R-A-S-I alternatives, it is possible that an actor has no assigned behavior opposite a particular type of activity, and this situation should be indicated by a dash (—).

Completion of the horizontal line gives one a *de facto modus operandi* for handling that particular class of task and its associated roles. Completion of a responsibility chart for all of the tasks relevant to the interfaces between departments or organizations and reading down a column vertically reveals the consensus role description of a particular actor on all those matters in which he or she is interdependent with other roles.

Some Further Guidelines in the Process

1. If an item has several A's, e.g., one R, six A's, one S, and one I, undoubtedly it will be very difficult to accomplish that task. For example, one organization decided to increase its benefits plan for management. The plan was agreed to by all levels of the organization; the board approved it, and the compensation people were told to install the plan. Nine months later, the plan was still not in. A responsibility-charting exercise indicated that each of the major profit centers had defined itself as having an A because it was an independent profit center with a budget commitment to the center. Because this new program required investment of funds not budgeted, each profit center's manager felt it was his or her choice to decide whether or not to institute the program this year or next year. It did not take long for the managing director to indicate, and for the profit center managers to see, that S rather than A was the appropriate

symbol to describe the profit center's role. Then the program got instituted very quickly.

2. Depending on who is filling out the chart, one might find a skewing of A's under the senior executive. Subordinate managers tend to give their bosses more A's than in fact the bosses want. It is desirable to try to minimize the number of A's for any task if one wishes to facilitate the accomplishment of the task.

3. The decision about who can allocate a letter to a role can be tricky. In one situation, for example, the management group decided that first-line supervisors in the production organization should be held accountable for weekly scrap losses and various other things and should have timely information about their progress toward their objectives and organization standards. However, the controller's department, which was part of the general headquarters, refused to develop and introduce a new cost-accounting system. The department's requirements for accounting systems were focused primarily on the needs of the top of the organization, the tax people, etc., and another system would have to be added in order to provide this new type of information. The department felt that as the top financial resource, it should have responsibility for deciding whether or not such a system, with the attendant costs, would be introduced.

At a responsibility-charting session, it became clear that the department had defined itself as having an A, whereas others lower in the organization felt strongly that the department should have an S—that it should be required to produce the system. At the meeting, the general manager supported those who were arguing for the S on the basis that the task required it. This changed the basis for making decisions from hierarchy position to task accomplishment.

Some Applications

Illustration 1: A Change in Structure.   A large consumer company identified with a particular product orientation decided to "go to market" in a different way. Previously the company had sold its product, which was used in interior decorating, through specialty stores. Instead of being known as a single-product company, the company now wanted to be known as a decorating company. This meant changing the products in the stores, changing the relationship of the franchised stores to the corporation, differentiating the various types of buyers—housewives, contractors, etc.—and providing outlets for customers' different needs.

The prechange organization was a marketing-sales-functional organization. All selling was done in the geographic regions under the direction of division and, ultimately, regional salesmanagers. Plants made products on demand from the different regions. The technical-service organization made the special blends of products required by the sales organization.

The company's top management felt that given the new marketing plan and corporate image, a new organizational structure was needed. Accordingly, the sales organization was maintained, but purely as a selling organization. Product managers were created within the marketing organization and were given worldwide responsibility for sales in their particular product or market area. Also created were product-technical managers, who came from the technical organization but also had a product or business orientation. People in the new technical-service role would now receive all of their instructions from the product-technical director rather than from the sales organization.

Everyone in the organization, with the exception of the production and finance organizations, now had a new role, a new set of task responsibilities, and new relationships. Much confusion could be expected.

The strategy for dealing with the confusion was to conduct a series of *responsibility-charting conferences*. The first two-day conference focused on the new roles—the product managers from marketing, the technical-product managers, and the top of the organization, i.e., the directors of marketing, manufacturing, technical and finance, and the group vice-president. After opening remarks by the group vice-president, the participants proceeded to do a responsibility-charting exercise. They identified areas of decision and activities that needed to be done, made a list of the actors, and then assigned behaviors to these actors. Because the top of the organization was also present, the assigned behavior could be "reality-tested" right then. The output of the two days was a "map" of the general *modus operandi* as seen by the top management and the occupants of the new roles.

Next, the two sets of roles in marketing—sales and product management—and the two sets of technical roles—product management and technical service—met to work through responsibilities and to assign behaviors for their roles in the new setup. Difficulties arising with the earlier models and maps were resolved by the top-management group that had attended the first workshops. The results were then distributed to everybody and became the basis for work.

The change, a massive one involving several thousand managers, was in effect. People were operating in their new roles within six weeks of the announcement of the change. The process of having all of the key people sit down together and develop the new *modus operandi* was credited by most as having a significant effect on the efficiency of the change.

Illustration 2: An Interface Problem.   The regional headquarters of a major oil company had been working for a couple of years on a different kind of franchise relationship with some of the company's gas station owners. The problem was complex, and there had been all sorts of misunderstandings, conflicts, slowdowns, and differences of emphasis between staff areas. The top management—the managing director, director of marketing, director of operations, and director of finance—were concerned about this issue because it was a matter of significant investment and cost, but they had been unable to resolve it.

At a meeting held for another purpose with the top group, the directors mentioned the difficulties they were having with this particular franchise problem. It was suggested that they do a responsibility-charting exercise on the problem, which they did. As a result, they discovered that they did not have a consensus about the location of different types of responsibilities and behaviors. This problem was relatively easy to work through.

By coincidence, the next day one of the authors was meeting with the operating management (about 40) of the same organization in a development meeting. As part of the content, we chose to describe responsibility charting and suggested that they take the franchise case, with which they were all very familiar, and do a responsibility-charting exercise on it. The population was divided into eight groups, all of which were to work on this problem. The groups came up with different results, although the patterns were similar. A significant fact to the consultant was that practically all of the patterns were different from the one that top management had produced the day before. It then was suggested that they take the results of their exercise and meet with a member of the board of directors to compare notes.

From this meeting, several things became obvious. (1) There was a gap in communication between the levels. (2) They needed the top management to expedite the change. (3) The distance between top management and top operating management was dysfunctional for issues of this kind.

Faced with the objective assignments of behavior in the responsibility charting, people were able to work with the issue as a problem rather than as an issue of management style or role conflict. The problem on which they had been working for two years was resolved in four weeks.

Illustration 3: Responsibility Allocation.   In a large medical school, the curriculum and teaching had been based on the various disciplines, e.g., biochemistry, medicine, surgery. Thus students took courses in the various technologies, in addition to their field work.

The faculty decided to add in to the discipline-based teaching some core courses built around types of delivery. One such course was primary care, meaning the stand-up, early-contact type of care. In this type of course, the teaching faculty came from various departments, such as pediatrics, medicine, psychology, psychiatry, etc.

Program directors appointed for the core program began recruiting faculty for their courses, but encountered considerable resistance from some of the department heads. The program directors, as well as some of the department heads, felt considerable frustration, and they brought a number of these problems and differences to the dean for resolution.

In searching for a better way of resolving these kinds of issues, the key program directors and department heads were exposed to the responsibility-charting technique. In a two-day exercise, they worked through the responsibilities and assigned behaviors of each role as it related to the handling of faculty assignments, rewards, changes in curriculum, etc. The result was to significantly reduce the dean's arbitration activity, provide clarity for the total faculty about decision making in the various areas, and provide agreed on methods of operation for handling these types of issues.

Summary

When interface problems produce role confusion about who does what to whom, traditional methods, such as more specific job descriptions, mediation by the boss, or separating the protagonists, tend to be unsatisfactory. A process that allows participants in a complex interface to sit down together and determine the best assigned role behavior for the various participants in different classes of tasks tends to produce positive change as well as more satisfaction. *Responsibility charting* is one method that has had a number of effective applications in dealing with this issue.

SUMMARY

In this chapter, we have looked at three kinds of changes—changes in relation to the environment, changes in structure, and changes in the way work is done—which we see as becoming increasingly prevalent in organizations. We have described and discussed some specific techniques and methods that are being used to attack these problems. Like previously developed methods, none of these is a panacea, but all three suggest that a process or method that allows for joint problem solving and planning may be the best way of developing a strategy for changes of this kind.

7
MONITORING AND EVALUATING CHANGE

One of the most difficult issues confronting executive management involved in the planning and management of change in complex organizations is how to undertake an assessment of the change effort. At some point in many change efforts, the following types of questions are raised by those managing the change:

1. How will (do) we know that the change effort will be (has been) worthwhile?

2. Will (has) the change effort work(ed)?

3. How will (do) we know how much of the outcome is the result of the change effort?

4. How do we know the new state will be maintained?

5. How do we monitor the change?

Although these types of questions are important and represent a high concern with evaluation, too often evaluation of the change is glossed over. This is partly due to a lack of serious consideration of evaluation issues in the early stages of the change and/or to the lack of *measures* developed to use as criteria against which to evaluate effects of interventions. Also, the informal evidence of success (or lack of success) is sometimes expected to be fairly obvious, thus making formal evaluation effort seem unnecessary.

In this chapter, we look at the effects of a change effort and provide a general overview of what is possible. In considering some of the issues involved in developing a plan for evaluating a change effort, our emphasis will be on outlining *how* one might begin to go about securing answers to the questions cited above. We will first look at the multiple functions of evaluation and then at a few of the organizational pitfalls in evaluation processes.

A DEFINITION OF EVALUATION

As a working definition of evaluation for this book, we propose the following. Evaluation is that set of *planned,* information-gathering, and analysis activities undertaken to provide those responsible for the management of the change with a satisfactory assessment of the effects and/or progress of the change effort.

A key phrase in this definition is "satisfactory assessment." Implicit in the term "satisfactory" is the allowance for less than perfect or ideal. Also implicit is the notion of choice. If the management need is to know how the change effort is progressing or what's happened, a range of evaluation options is available, each of which can more or less satisfy that need. The range of options runs from making no assessment, to undertaking a comprehensive, rigorous, "scientifically correct" evaluation. The point is that evaluation need not be seen as an "all or nothing" choice.

The other key word in this definition is *planned.* Evaluation is often glossed over and viewed as an add-on or extracurricular activity of a change effort. If evaluation is viewed as such and generally undertaken as an afterthought, it is predictable that the quality of the information or the cost of the evaluation, or both, are likely to be unsatisfactory. If the questions posed at the beginning of this chapter represent issues of concern for management, evaluation activities should be a planned and integrated part of the change effort. Like the interventions, evaluation should be considered early in the process of change.

DEVELOPING AN EVALUATION PLAN

In considering the evaluation of a planned change effort, the following require attention and decision on the part of the change manager:

1. *Clearly* defining the purpose or functions served by the evaluation;

2. Determining the types of information needed by the management and the appropriate sources of that information;

3. Choosing data-collection methods and considering time and resource constraints;

4. Deciding when to evaluate—timing of data gathering and data review by management.

Evaluation for What Purpose?

One of the major traps for organizations in evaluating change in complex systems is the failure to clarify and prioritize the purposes of the evaluation. Without clearly specifying the primary purpose, criteria such as ease of data gathering and the use of "interesting" questions rather than a search for critical information can become paramount. If those managing the change can specify a primary purpose—identify those questions of prime concern—and then list the kinds of information needed to achieve that purpose, an efficient plan can be developed for evaluation. If other purposes or information are desirable, choices can be made by applying relevant *secondary* criteria about whether to include those issues in the evaluation. Let us look briefly at several relevant purposes of evaluation.

1. *Total-system performance review.*   Here the focus is on reviewing the *outcomes* of the change effort. Such a review would involve comparing the organizational outcomes of the change with the goals or desired conditions established prior to the effort. The key questions to be answered would include the following. To what extent has the desired condition been achieved? In what areas is further change required? What, if any, unanticipated consequences have resulted from the change effort? What are the current attitudes of personnel (systemwide) toward the current organizational condition? How satisfied is top management with the current and likely near-future organizational condition? How well can the system now function relative to accomplishment of the organization's mission?

2. *Monitoring the effects of specific interventions.*   It can also be useful to look at the effects of unique interventions in the change effort. Recognizing that the intervention strategy developed probably

involves a series of *interdependent* interventions or one major intervention with a number of interrelated goals, it then becomes important to assess whether a given action has produced the anticipated outcomes.

An important characteristic of large-system change interventions is that often the "action" is like a pebble thrown into the water. A small intervention (a pebble) in a large system (a lake) can have far-reaching effects (sending ripples to the far shore). Such interventions may be highly desirable and cost-effective. However, since interventions in large systems are often planned and managed at some "distance" from the point of direct action, it is important to carefully consider the cost-benefit factors.

It is often desirable to carefully monitor at least key interventions and their effects, both direct and secondary. If an intervention results in a significant gap between the expected outcome and the actual result or if there are unanticipated "ripple" effects in other parts of the system, *immediate remedial action* may be needed. A consciously planned and administered surveillance process of specific interventions can help get the timely information needed to inform management of whether to move forward with the strategy as planned or modify or "correct the direction."

3. *Energy and goal-directed tension.* One of the problems in change management is maintaining a sufficient level of positive tension in the system to produce sustained energy and motivation for the change effort. The evaluation process can be used as a mechanism for producing such an *energy system*. In this case, the formal evaluation itself is an *intervention*. By making the organization aware that evaluation will be an integral part of the change effort and specifying publicly when, where, and how evaluation interventions will be performed, it is possible to *create or maintain energy* in the system toward the change while simultaneously producing information on how the effort is progressing.

The choice of when and where to intervene is obviously important to the issue of using evaluation to produce energy. Often the optimal time for an evaluation is at a natural lull in the change effort, i.e., when a major activity (intervention) has been completed (a goal achieved) and there is a lapse before any further major intervention will occur. At such a point, there is a tendency for "relaxation" or lowered energy. The anticipation of any evaluation can mobilize energy.

One of the potential purposes of an evaluation of a change effort is to provide the information needed to use the change effort as a *learning experience*—to analyze and review the change effort so as to learn about the organization's problem-handling and management mechanisms. The diagnosis and planning stages of the change process provide an opportunity for examining past experience and results. An integral part of the change project could be an examination and change in the organization's problem handling or management. Through a relatively small additional investment in time and effort, the change effort could do double duty—resolving the "problem" at hand *and* providing an opportunity to develop, practice, and evaluate improved organizational problem-handling styles.

What Information and from Whom?
Sources of Data and Targets of Evaluation

Here the issue is identifying the appropriate sources of information and the types of information about the organization needed to inform management of the effect of the change. The types of questions which should be addressed are as follows:

1. What organizational variables are of primary concern?
   a) attitudes—toward organizational goals, morale, etc.
   b) organizational processes—communication, decision making, problem solving, conflict, management, etc.
   c) organizational structure—clarity of role responsibilities, reward system, reporting relationships, etc.
   d) organizational outcomes—productivity, sales, turnover, etc.

2. Who in the system possesses the kinds of information desired?

3. Who will use the information produced?

4. Is there a plan to feed back the data provided to the sources of the data? To the whole organization?

A universal phenomenon about feedback is that when people are asked for their view, opinion, or perspective on an issue *and* when they know that others are also being asked to respond, they have a high need to know and compare their own response(s) with those of the others. When satisfaction of this need is denied, especially without reasonable explanation, the result is generally frustration and some resentment (negative energy). Thus it is important for management to plan a means of *feeding back* some form of the data *or* giving the sources a clear and reasonable explanation for why such feedback is impossible or impractical.

Choice of the targets of evaluation and location of the appropriate sources of data should follow from management's definition of the "purpose" of the evaluation. Examination of the organizational variables mentioned earlier should provide the change managers with information needed to answer the questions of primary concern about how the change is progressing. Similarly, the information sources should be chosen on the basis of providing the "best" information —valid, timely, and relevant—on the variables of interest.

How Do We Get the Information?

Methods.   An integral part of the evaluation plan should be specifying *how* the needed information will be gathered and analyzed. We shall briefly outline the issues which should be considered in choosing methods and list some of the options available.

1. *Choice of data-collection methods.*   Numerous data-collection methods are available, e.g., interviews, questionnaires, observations, organizational records, and operations reporting forms. Each method has its own relative advantages and disadvantages concerning the ease and speed of use, cost, and quality of the data provided.

2. *Time and resource constraints.*   In choosing the appropriate method, the change management's priorities about time versus money versus quality of the information should be seriously considered. For example, how quickly is the information needed? If the *purpose* of the evaluation is to get information on the *effect* of a specific intervention in order to determine whether to continue the effort as planned or to undertake "corrective" action, it is obviously necessary to get the needed assessment information to decision makers quickly. In such a case, an elaborate, time-consuming data-gathering effort would be inappropriate. On the other hand, if the evaluation purpose is to assess the *overall state* of the system after a systemwide change effort,

comprehensiveness of the data, not time, may be the overriding concern.

Timing.   The choice of when to review or monitor the change—at the "completion" of the effort, at regular intervals during the transition, or at specific points during major planned interventions—needs to be decided in terms of the purpose of the evaluation. Usually, there are *two* sets of timing decisions to be made. One involves the question of when to *collect* the information; the other, when management should *review* the information collected. It is helpful to separate these two issues and to make choices about data-collection timing based on a determination of when the best needed data are available and when the best time is to *review*.

Who Should Do What?: The Role of Staff or Outside Specialists

Several of the issues outlined above may require specialized knowledge and skill, e.g., selection and design of data collection and analysis methods. Similarly, the actual collection of the needed information will likely require significant time and labor to carry out the activity. Management must decide how to use staff or specialized resources to ensure that the necessary tasks are performed. This choice is one of deciding whether to give responsibility for design, implementation, and analysis of the evaluation to staff experts or to use those experts as consultants and *assistants* to management (to provide technical assistance) in carrying out those tasks. Though subtle, this distinction can be important. It is a distinction based on who will control or be responsible for managing the "production" of management decision-making information—the change managers or the staff experts. Usually, if the information desired is deemed important, management *should* be integrally involved in its production. This is not to say that the management should design questionnaires, decide on methods of data analysis, conduct interviews, etc.; rather, management needs to be actively involved in decisions about what questions should be asked, where (from whom) information should be collected, and how (methods, resources needed, support required) the evaluation should be conducted so as to provide the information needed.

Our definition of evaluation as those activities whose primary purpose is to provide the change management with a satisfactory assessment on the progress of the change effort highlights the need for management inputs on what type of information will be satisfactory and raises the issue of what management must do to ensure a satisfactory assessment. One consequence of not having adequate managerial personnel involved in the *management* of the evaluation is increased risk that the information collected may not satisfactorily inform management decision making.

SOME WARNINGS: ORGANIZATIONAL PITFALLS IN EVALUATION

1. *Clarifying employees' perceived linkage between the rewards system and evaluation.*   For many people in organizations, evaluation can be a threatening experience, especially if their previous experiences with evaluation have been solely to determine promotions and/or financial raises. In such systems, the learned response is "hide failure and stress successes, for that's where the goodies are." Organizational members learn that there is no payoff for admitting mistakes; in fact, they often develop sophisticated mechanisms for hiding them. In attempting to evaluate the change effort, requests for data can be met with the same fear of admitting failure. The result is often the production of invalid data about the current state of affairs.

The problem confronting the change managers is how to ensure that the information produced in the evaluation is valid. The following few guidelines can improve the likelihood of getting valid data. First, make the purpose of the evaluation explicit and stress the importance of getting valid data. Second, make a clear and explicit distinction between evaluation of the change effort and evaluation of individuals' performance. For example, a statement to the effect that it is the entire organization and the change effort, *not* individuals and groups, that is being evaluated can help to clarify the issue. Third, to the extent possible, allow individuals and groups to remain anonymous. Finally, stress that information is being sought about *both* successes and problem areas; this can help to temper any tendency to focus on one of the extremes.

The important point here is that for many organizations and their members, evaluation of the system will be a new experience. The more novel this experience is, the less likely the organization will be able to comfortably produce evidence that reflects negatively on its subsystems. If one accepts that these dynamics may be operating and recognizes the change management's dependence on the information produced, it becomes important to develop conscious plans to improve the likelihood that the evaluation will produce valid information.

2. *Information overload.*   In designing evaluation or monitoring processes, people tend to try to get as much information as possible on how things are progressing. The assumption that "more is better" can hold several traps and result in serious consequences, however. First, if the information being gathered comes from members of the organization involved in the change, the requirement to provide "more" information can detract attention and energy from the change. Second, there are crucial questions about why management needs the information and what will be done with it. If the answers to such questions are vague and general, management will probably get bogged down trying to sort through all the data they come to realize was unnecessary. Third, the cost of "more" is higher, and although "while we're at it, we can get this and that for little extra cost" seems reasonable, the aggregate data-handling costs (psychological and financial) for both staff and management can increase quickly.

If the evaluation is well thought out, i.e., if decisions are made about what is to be evaluated and why, simplistic strategies, such as "let's get all the data we can," can be examined as to their appropriateness. Some thought and planning and a few critical pieces of data can be much more useful than a truckload of data analyzed in every conceivable way. The key is to ask *"why"* when it is proposed that "we should get information about . . . ; it might be interesting and it won't cost anything," rather than the easy response, "sure, why not?"

EVALUATION OF PLANNED CHANGE: A CASE ILLUSTRATION

A change effort was planned in a large, national consumer-products firm. The project involved changing the way allocation of sales orders to manufacturing and the distribution of goods was handled nationwide. The change was expected to directly affect all manufacturing plants, almost all of the sales force, and much of the order-processing people in marketing; about 2000 employees would have their jobs changed in some way.

The company had numerous manufacturing plants spread across the country. Each plant was capable of manufacturing numerous products and received its production orders from the corporate vice-president of manufacturing. The effort was geared to changing the way products orders were sent to manufacturing so as to reduce time-delays between receipt of an order and delivery to the customer.

Previously the sales organization received an order from either the field salespeople or a customer, made a weekly compilation of total orders received by product and by geographic region, and submitted that report to corporate manufacturing. Manufacturing would then make production assignments to the various plants. The job of the manufacturing plants was to meet the production assignments received; if schedule slippages or problems occurred, corporate manufacturing was notified, and either new schedules were assigned or production assignments were transferred to other plants.

The change would have sales order–processing personnel provide daily data concerning orders received, directly to all manufacturing plants, which would "accept" these orders from sales. If more than one plant "accepted" a sales order, the sales management would decide which of the plants would get the order. If after three days no plant had accepted an order from sales, the order would be sent to corporate manufacturing, which would assign the order to a plant. In such cases, a formula would assign a shared cost to both the manufacturing plant and sales. A bonus system based on the performance of both sales and manufacturing as a group was established.

Purpose of the Evaluation

Management wanted to evaluate the change. They selected the primary evaluation purpose as identifying the *types of problems encountered* in the early stages of change, with the intent that the evaluation would guide the design of actions to eliminate such problems.

Determining the Types of Information Needed and Sources of Information

In a top-management discussion focusing on anticipating the types of problems which might occur, it became clear that problems were likely to exist throughout the target system, across functions, and up and down the hierarchy. The following types of problems were anticipated.

1. Plant managers will "accept" only local orders, to reduce their distribution costs and will therefore leave customers less centrally located without product or with delayed delivery.

2. Friction may develop between sales and the manufacturing plants.

3. There is likely to be increased confusion about the role of corporate manufacturing and its relationship to the plants.

4. There could be confusion and problems in the plants about scheduling and allocation of product to production. Plant personnel may not be adequately trained to handle the new responsibilities being placed on them.

5. What will happen to customer relations during this change? There may be mistakes and mixups of orders and deliveries during the early stages of the change. The delivery people and salespeople will have to take customers' complaints resulting from manufacturing's and order processing's mistakes.

The management listed the types of potential problems, their likely locations (departments, interfaces, regions, etc.), and the types of information which would indicate the existence and nature of the problems. This last list included: (1) the state of relationships among plants and sales, plants and corporate manufacturing, customers and salesforce, etc.; (2) clarity of new roles and responsibility within plants and the order-processing department; (3) customer satisfaction; (4) time- and costs-savings measures in order processing; (5) production-scheduling problems at plants and the amount and types of orders being sent to corporate manufacturing; (6) morale of personnel; (7) capability of plant personnel to handle new responsibilities; and (8) trends in problem handling, e.g., an increase or decrease in problems and whether or not they are being worked on, ignored, or neglected.

A cross-section of the entire organization was needed to provide data. Also, since the evaluation was to highlight opportunities for *"remedial"* action, timeliness of the information was a relevant factor.

Choice of Data Collection and Analysis Methods: Role of Staff

Top management called in staff personnel from its administrative services group and outlined the desired purpose and types of information it needed for the evaluation. The staff was asked to help management decide how to design and implement the evaluation. The staff gave an overview of the pros and cons of various methods of data collection and analysis, sampling procedures, etc.

After reviewing alternative methods of data collection, the decision was made to use questionnaires. Because of the large number of people and sites involved and the need to have a relatively quick turnaround of the data from collection to action if needed, management felt that questionnaires would be the most satisfactory data-gathering method. Further, although management felt that its list of information and potential problems was comprehensive and could be easily converted into a series of "check the appropriate box" questions, a few open-ended questions, e.g., "Please describe any other problems *you* have encountered in changing to the new procedures and operations" were included. Management hoped that these open-ended questions would identify any unanticipated problems left unaddressed by the structured-response questions. Based on the recommendation of the staff, a random sample of 200 of the 2000 employees involved was selected to fill out the questionnaires. Finally, *all* management people in the target systems were sent questionnaires, as it was felt that most problems would be brought to their attention.

The questionnaires were designed so that responses could be keypunched directly from the completed questionnaires, and analysis programs were written to perform the analysis. The analysis plan called for computer processing of the check-off items, whereas the open-ended responses were processed (categorized and interpreted) individually.

Deciding When to Evaluate

On the issue of *when* to collect the information, management decided that one month after the structural changes had been initiated would allow adequate time for the people in the system to resolve some of the problems encountered on their own, yet frustrations resulting from unresolved problems would not yet have become acute.

Staff were assigned responsibility for collecting and analyzing the information. Management set a date for a day and a half meeting, at which the change management would review the data and decide on appropriate actions.

Clarifying the Organization's Perceptions of the Evaluation

As part of the evaluation plan, top management prepared a statement to all employees in the target system stating that a random sample of them would be asked to participate in the evaluation of the change to date. It also stated that management was very committed to seeing that the desired change was accomplished. Further, the statement noted management's awareness that such a change was difficult for everyone and likely to cause problems and that these problems should be identified and resolved. It stressed that it was more important at this point to know what problems existed and their consequences than to hear how well things were going. Thus management emphasized candidness and accuracy over evidence of success. Finally, the statement promised that a summary report of the findings and an outline of next steps would appear in the company newspaper.

Much of the groundwork for this evaluation was done during the planning stages of the change effort. The evaluation itself—from distribution of the questionnaires to development of new remedial interventions—took a little over a month. The evaluation and its feedback through the company newspaper was a powerful intervention itself.

Consideration of and decisions about evaluation should occur in the *early planning* stages of the change project. When management has defined the organization's goals, criteria against which to measure results should be discussed and operationalized as part of the planning of change. These criteria can then become the yardstick against which to measure outcomes and progress and can also be used as guides in the selection of specific interventions.

SUMMARY

In this chapter, we have listed a number of the key issues and important questions which must be answered in developing an appropriate evaluation plan. Clearly, the issues surrounding evaluation are complex, but we have found that by developing a plan for evaluation which is well integrated with the change effort, the change management can provide itself with information which can help significantly in the management of the change.

An effective evaluation plan should have the following elements.

1. Clarity and agreement about the purpose or priorities for the evaluation;

2. Determination of required information and selection of appropriate sources of the needed information;

3. Decision about who will receive the data from the evaluation (users and feedback to sources);

4. Decision on when to evaluate and selection of data-collection and analysis method(s);

5. Determination of resources required and available, selection of required resources, and clarification of the role of staff.

The decisions about required activities which define the evaluation plan should be part of the process, or *activity plan,* for the change effort. This plan should spell out who will do what, when, and where.

8
THE BALANCE BETWEEN STABILITY AND CHANGE

As we said at the beginning of this book, the executive manager is simultaneously managing current operations, planning and designing the future state of the organization, and managing the process of getting from the present to the future. Major changes in programs, organizational structure, relationships to other organizations, mergers, priorities—all require large amounts of energy, specialized management structures, new procedures, and perhaps change of rewards.

When a change is "completed," people in the organization experience reaching a major goal. At this point people are probably feeling happy, relaxed, and there is a release of energy. When one achieves a goal, tension is reduced. People rarely work harder the day after achieving a major goal; they may feel better and like their organization more, but they are unlikely to be highly *energized*. This "hangover" effect usually occurs after a major goal achievement. The situation is often reinforced in organizations by a change in the structure; after achieving the new state, the change management reverts to operating management, attending to things other than the change.

It is a common experience to see a team work together day and night to create a new plant with new working conditions and increased quality of life. When the new, highly productive plant opens, people are highly motivated, and the interdisciplinary team of engineering, plant management, and personnel and other staff who helped make this possible is appreciated. These people then depart for other places to work on new projects. The management of the plant now settles down to "managing the operation." Six months or a year later, the excitement is over; the operation is routine. The decisions that were being made by the development team are probably now in the hands of the shift supervisors. The plant manager's attention is on other things. People in the organization experience stability but not much challenge, particularly if the tasks under the new state tend to be routine. The attention and energy involved in establishing the dynamic new situation have dissipated and are now placed elsewhere. The result is often a reversion to the prechange, old ways of operating.

To avoid such a relapse, which occurs in not only new plants, but also in changes requiring new ways of work or new decisions or any major change, the executive management of the organization must recognize that the new state is also "dynamic" and probably won't be the same in a few years hence. The executive management needs to *behave* in ways that build in a continuing *monitoring* and *improvement* process *as part of doing business*. If managerial behavior indicates that the change is *over*, people will settle into the new condition.

There is a dilemma here. One wishes to reduce the ambiguity and confusion that existed during the "getting from here to there" state. Concurrently, however, energy can be fully mobilized only if conscious attention is given to a continuous process of checking "how are we doing," i.e., setting goals and priorities for *improving* the condition.

In this brief chapter, we want to look at a few tested mechanisms for maintaining and updating change.

CONDITIONS FOR MAINTAINING A CHANGE

Some of the conditions necessary for maintenance of change are as follows. First, management must pay conscious attention to the "continuous *transition*." Second, explicit processes or procedures for setting priorities for improvement should be instituted. Third, there should be systematic and continual processes of feedback. Fourth, the reward system should reward people for time and energy spent on these processes.

SOME MECHANISMS FOR
MAINTAINING AND UPDATING CHANGE

When a change in organization structure, leadership, rewards, or ways of work has occurred and the process is operating, there is a need for (1) specific mechanisms to provide management with information on *how* it is operating and the effects of its operations, and (2) mechanisms to provide information to people widely dispersed in the system, who may be concerned with only parts of the change. Perhaps the most important single requirement for continued vitality is an effective feedback and information system that lets people in the organization know where they are in relation to continuous changing of desired states. Some feedback systems that are used fairly frequently are described below.

1. *Periodic team meetings.*   Every six months or so, management groups, significant department heads, or new management systems could meet to review the team's state vis à vis the new organizational condition or goals and to set goals and goal priorities for the next short-term period. Although the need for such meetings may not be obvious, having them and "forcing" the members to think through what they have done and what has happened since the last meeting and where they are going in the next intermediate period is itself a tension-producing, goal-directed process.

2. *Organization sensing meetings.*   This is a process whereby the top manager or managers of the organization meet regularly with a sample of employees from different parts of the organization and in a variety of different configurations in order to keep information flowing about the current state of the system. Specifically, the head of a department, company, or area and his or her management colleagues set up the "design" for a series of regular meetings, e.g., once a week for a year. The composition of the membership of these meetings is determined by a formula that will ensure good, thorough coverage of the information which is widely held throughout the system.

For example, in one large system with about 16,000 personnel, the president held biweekly sensing meetings. The different combinations of participants at each meeting were as follows:

a) a group of people doing similar jobs at the same level, e.g., secretaries, line operators, or maintenance personnel;

b) a diagonal slice of organization management, e.g., department heads, section heads, first-line supervisors;

c) a vertical slice across management-labor lines, e.g., the same as (b), including the technicians or hourly people;

d) a diagonal slice of an organizational unit, e.g., one director, a department head from a different division, a section head from a different section, a supervisor from a different section, etc.

e) a sample from the same "level" of the hierarchy but with different functions, e.g., a secretary, a technician, some process operators, etc.

These meetings were scheduled for one hour in the president's conference room. Prior to the meeting, the group's members (selected by the local personnel and/or management people) would meet with a staff person from the corporate personnel group just to meet one another and begin to think about what to discuss with the president. After adjourning to the conference room, the president would ask, "How's life?"

The group could talk about anything, and the meetings would be tape recorded in order to allow the president to listen more carefully. The president might use the meeting to check a communications question, such as how many people in the room know that the organization got an award for excellence last week, or that a new customer had just been lost or gained, or that a new invention had just been patented, or that a reorganization occurred in the engineering department.

A significant rule was that whatever data came up in the meetings would not be used to punish anyone in the organization. Instead, the information would be used to communicate the general tone of the meeting to the managers who were not at the meeting, since part of this process is an intentional bypass of intervening levels of management.

After the conference, the president would share the kinds of things heard at the meeting with senior colleagues at their next staff meeting and would identify areas that needed to be "looked into." Senior officials would then use these data to guide the development of remedial corrective action or new communications processes or procedures.

3. *Periodic intergroup meetings.*   If the change has resulted in the establishment of a new relationship, such as the introduction of a brand management interfacing with a line sales-management group, and if new roles require work allocations to be made, it is extremely useful for either the total membership of each of the functions or at least a representative group to meet regularly to identify what's working, what needs more work, and why. In addition to clarifying work procedures, such meetings, as a form of forced collaboration, require the subunits to stay in contact with one another. If the process and the meetings are effectively managed, they can have the effect of "teaching" the group ways of effectively collaborating.

4. *Renewal conferences.*   Several organizations have a practice of managers, often with their spouses, going to a "retreat" for a few days. Here their agenda is to examine company priorities, determine topics to be discussed in future planning meetings, share perceptions as individuals in the management group, identify and discuss new forces in the environment, and examine what's happened in their work and in their relationships that needs review. They have found that this informal, but with an agenda, two- or three-day session can result in significant improvement of both the process and effectiveness of the group's planning.

5. *Goal-directed performance review.*   Another continuous process that helps provide information on change is to be sure that semiannual or annual performance reviews focus on both past performance and setting priorities, as well as program goals and targets for the next short-term period. If an effective, goal-directed planning process is in place, one generally finds that the organization is alive, energized, and relatively clear about its priorities. The use of performance appraisal or review process to reinforce goal-directed planning procedures establishes a compatibility between the organization's reward system and desired ways of working.

6. *Periodic visits from outside consultants.*   It is sometimes desirable to have a consultant meet with the management group or the relevant team on a regular basis, such as every six months, to help the group "take the temperature" of the state of the change. The most significant contribution the consultant makes is being there, not what he or she does. We have found that insisting on such review visits for at least a year or so after a major change intervention "forces" the

organization leadership to have follow-up meetings. It forces them to look at the promises they made at the last meeting, to review progress, and to do some conscious thinking about priority planning for the future.

The key point here is that each of the processes above is a conscious, repeated way of working which is added to the existing job requirements of members of the organization.

7. *Rewards.*   The six activities just described, although logically sound, may very well be resisted if key members of the organization don't see their immediate usefulness, don't believe that they still warrant high-priority time, or don't sense that participants are *supported* for spending energy this way.

One of the common characteristics of a major change is that during the change itself, it is quite legitimate for people to take time off to plan or be on project teams or study groups. Once the change is in place, people are expected to get back to their "real" jobs. Activities such as periodic team meetings, if not perceived as fundamental work of the organization, will soon be relegated to the category of extra-curricular activities. This occurrence is dysfunctional for continuing the organization's vitality. For example, the amount of energy involved in organization sensing meetings is significant. For the chief executive to try it once or twice and then give it up is worse than if it had never been tried. The message in that case is that this is a technique of going through some motions of information collecting; the desired message is that this activity is part of the process of connecting the parts of the organization.

Performance reviews should explicitly include some evaluation of performance in carrying out these change-management processes, if maximum involvement is to be achieved. Linkage of the rewards system to stability and maintenance of change activities, such as mentioned in the goal-directed performance-review process, provides organizational members with clear signals of management commitment and emphasis.

SUMMARY

When a major change has been accomplished, it is important for the executive management of whatever the system that has been changed to maintain an active interest and provide leadership behavior for ensuring that the new state does not become ossified. A variety of mechanisms can be used for consciously taking the temperature of the organization, setting priorities for short-term improvements and review, and rewarding people for doing this so it is seen as real work rather than as activity in addition to work. All of these procedures can increase the likelihood that the efforts and investments involved in creating the change will pay off for the organization.

9
DEVELOPING TRENDS IN PLANNED CHANGE

As a final thought, we are going to take authors' liberty to prognosticate the likely conditions in the late 1970s and early 1980s both outside and inside the organization.

OUTSIDE ENVIRONMENT

1. The environment will remain complex. Managers will have to respond to multiple constituencies making competing demands relatively independent of one another. There will be less clarity of "ownership" of the private enterprise. Managers will continuously have to make decisions about whether to please owners, public opinion, government.

2. Values will play an increasingly important part in environmental pressures. Although they will vary up and down, depending on the immediate economic situation, the demands of minorities, women, consumer advocates, and environmental advocates are here to stay. These demands will be a force to be managed, certainly for the decade ahead.

Values concerning distribution of wealth will also be a significant force affecting organizations and their management. Managers will be required to balance the traditional concept of the private-enterprise organization as having a mission of producing wealth for its owners or wealth for society with the value emerging in many countries that the core mission of private enterprise is to provide employment and that wealth production is a function of providing employment.

3. Government intervention and (probably) control will increase. In many countries there will be more laws requiring boards of directors to be composed of both owners and employees. The power distribution among owners, professional managers, and the trade unions will undergo a variety of agonizing reappraisals and adjustments.

4. In spite of predictable high unemployment for the next few years, we predict that the high expectations held by entering employees will continue. Young college and advanced-degree graduates entering the work place are less and less likely to be choosing and entering their permanent career home and more and more likely to be choosing and entering a place which will provide meaningful rewards, both financial and intrinsic, in the very immediate future in return for their effort. They will expect to advance fairly quickly and/or be rewarded fairly significantly. When a 24-year-old masters student lacking significant work experience can immediately go into the marketplace at a starting salary of $20,000, it is not hard to understand why these high expectations exist.

5. Middle managers and midcareer managers will be changing their priorities. In an informal study of six companies, Beckhard (1977) found that of people in their midforties being actively considered for significant promotions to top operating management, 70 percent of those who reach the final selection were actively considering early retirement in their fifties.[1] These high-producing, high-potential people were not dissatisfied with the company, but rather were beginning to think about the last half of their lives and how to redistribute their energy so that they could achieve a better balance among family, firm, and personal needs.

6. We are likely to see a leveling out of the tremendous push from the 1950s for new technology. There will still be many introductions of

---

1   R. Beckhard, "Managerial Careers in Transition: Dilemmas and Directions," Chapter 7 in John Van Maaness, ed., *Organizational Careers: Some New Perspectives* (New York and London: Wiley, 1977), pp. 149–160.

new technology, but high creativity and high motivation will be the more significant competitive variables.

7. Although people coming into management from colleges and universities will have high expectations, we will probably find low expectations more characteristic of people entering the work force at lower-level jobs. Many people entering the work force are entering in order to get short-term rewards (money) and are unconcerned about the company's profit or product quality. Company loyalty for them is an irrelevant concept. Motivating these people to work productively is going to be a significant continuing problem. Activities connected with improvement of the quality of work—sociotechnical and open-systems experiments—are going to be very much needed.

INSIDE THE ORGANIZATION

1. There will be more multitask professionals, that is, people doing a variety of tasks. In research organizations, for example, more and more professionals will be asked to bridge their technology with a market orientation.

2. There will be more interface between work and the family. More people will be conscious of the relationship of their personal "matrix" of family and firm and will be working toward some kind of management of that interface. This will have implications for organizational managements in terms of personnel practices, reward systems, vacation and retirement policies, etc.

3. There will be more need for creative coping. The competitive or effective organization, product, or service will need to have strong capability for flexibility and adaptability in organizing work so that it creates and releases creative capacity.

4. The decreasing need for some roles, e.g., engineers, will provide an imbalance, certainly for the next few years, between skills possessed by college graduates and the organizational requirements for their utilization. This will probably produce some anxiety and difficulties for young people entering the market as well as for recruiters and organizational managers.

5. As Beckhard said in his earlier book in this series, there is a continuous need for synergizing the change technologies—organization development, information systems, systems dynamics, operations research—into a problem-focused area. Most present organizations still treat these areas as separate specialties. Staffs are rewarded for getting their technology or specialty into the system or monitoring it after it is in there. In the leading-edge organization, there will probably be a "department of the future" sitting "next door" to the chief executive officer. Members of this staff department will be planners and experts in information systems, applied behavioral science, change management, and operations research and systems analysis. These people will function as a technology transfer arm to the chief operating and policy officers, focusing on helping the organization move toward continued creative coping with the ever-changing conditions.

Considering the increasing complexity of the interaction among private, public, and government enterprises and the interaction between people's needs for worth and self-actualization, which place additional pressure on organization leaders to meet these as well as economic and general social demands, the case for conscious large-system planning, it seems to us, will continue to be self-evident.

6. There will be increasing concern about the quality of life and the quality of working life. There will be more experiments aimed at reorganizing, sometimes drastically, the whole nature of the way work is done or organizations are staffed, in order to provide more autonomy and more influence for people at all levels and organizations.

MANAGING PLANNED CHANGE: AN ART? A TECHNIQUE? A SCIENCE?

Large-system intervention is, and will probably continue to be, largely an art. But like an art, the "artist" needs to have *some* technology and *some* tools and experience in using them. The artist, painting on a canvas, has extensively studied form, graphics, and color mixes and relies on both experience and intuition to create the painting. The manager of the change process and the organization consultant who helps must both be judged on the "artistry" of their product. We have offered a few techniques, tools, and formulas to use as the base for these acts.

It is obvious that the process of intervention is complex. One of the biggest traps for large-system change efforts is the failure of organizational leaders to resist the temptation to rush through the planning process to get to the "action" stage. Although the pressures for results are often due to a need to eliminate the acute negative consequences of the problem, it has been our experience that a great portion of large-system change efforts failed because of a lack of understanding on the part of the organizational leadership of what the process of intervention and change involves. When the manager lacks an appreciation for and understanding of the complexity of the intervention process, it is predictable that the emphasis will be on "action" or results. Management must gain a basic understanding of the whats, hows, and whys of the intervention process and be able to recognize its developmental and interdependent nature as a necessary condition for success in planned change efforts.

Successful intervention in large systems is becoming more of a science than an art, but it is still not a cookbook process, nor is it ever likely to be. However, the utilization of systematic procedures and technologies in the planning and management of large systems change can only help.

We hope that this book has helped those involved in managing change in complex organizations, especially top organizational leaders, to understand the process of change or transition management better *and* to have a better idea of what is required to facilitate and improve that process.